Weeds of the West

Publisher

The Western Society of Weed Science in cooperation with the
Western United States Land Grant Universities
Cooperative Extension Services

Authors

Tom D. Whitson, Editor
Extension Weed Specialist, University of Wyoming

Larry C. Burrill
Extension Weed Specialist, Oregon State University

Steven A. Dewey
Extension Weed Specialist, Utah State University

David W. Cudney
Extension Weed Specialist, University of California at Riverside

B.E. Nelson
Herbarium Manager, Rocky Mountain Herbarium,
Department of Botany, University of Wyoming

Richard D. Lee
Extension Weed Specialist, New Mexico State University

Robert Parker
Extension Weed Scientist, Washington State University

5th Edition, 1999

For order information contact an Extension Bulletin Room of the
Western States Land Grant Universities
or
The Western Society of Weed Science
P.O. Box 963
Newark, CA 94560

UNIVERSITY OF
WYOMING

*Published in cooperation with the Western Society of Weed Science, the Western United States Land
Grant Universities Cooperative Extension Services and the*

Library of Congress Catalogue Card Number: 90-71566
ISBN: 0-941570-13-4
WSWS-001

Printed by

Pioneer of Jackson Hole, Jackson, Wyoming

Contributors

Jim Ansley
Texas Agricultural Experiment Station, Vernon, Texas

K. George Beck
Extension Weed Scientist, Colorado State University

Carl Bell
Extension Farm Advisor, Imperial County, California

Chris Boerboom
Extension Weed Specialist, Washington State University

John P. Chernicky
Plant Sciences Department, University of Arizona

LaRea J. Dennis
Assistant Curator of the Herbarium (Emeritus),
Botany and Plant Pathology Department, Oregon State University

John O. Evans
Professor of Weed Science, Utah State University

Peter K. Fay
Professor of Agronomy, Montana State University

Mark A. Ferrell
Pesticide Specialist, University of Wyoming

Kenneth A. French
Oregon Department of Agriculture

Robert B. Hawkes
Oregon Department of Agriculture

Daniel W. Kidder
Research and Development, Ciba Geigy Company, Morehead, Minnesota

Wayne I. Kobayashi
Department of Agriculture Chief, Chemical/Mechanical Control Section, State of Hawaii

Stephen D. Miller
Professor of Weed Science, University of Wyoming

Larry W. Mitich
Extension Weed Scientist, University of California-Davis

F.E. Northam
Research Associate, Weed Science, University of Idaho

Richard Old
Private Consultant, Pullman, Washington

Roy Reichenbach
Supervisor, Converse County Weed and Pest Control District, Douglas, Wyoming

Andy Sanders
Museum Scientist, Herbarium Curator, University of California-Riverside

Richard J. Shaw
Professor of Botany (Emeritus), Director of Intermountain Herbarium, Utah State University

Frank H. Smith
Professor (Emeritus), Botany and Plant Pathology Department, Oregon State University

Dean G. Swan
Extension Weed Scientist (Emeritus), Washington State University

Donald C. Thill
Professor of Weed Science, University of Idaho

Table of Contents

Introduction

Members of the Western Society of Weed Science determined that an identification book showing and describing important weed species in the western United States was needed.

Weeds discussed in this book were selected by weed scientists who are members of the Western Society of Weed Science. Weeds were selected because of their abundance, ability to reproduce, compete, and spread rapidly, as well as those that are toxic to livestock or humans. An attempt was made to include a representative cross-section of the common agronomic, rangeland, horticultural, and non-cropland weeds of the western United States. States included are from Montana to New Mexico to the Pacific Ocean, including Hawaii. If plants are not included in the publication contact your county extension agent or university herbarium for proper identification.

There are many ways to define a weed. The authors think the following accurately describes the criteria used for including plants in this book:

> *A plant that interferes with management objectives for*
> *a given area of land at a given point in time.*
>
> *– J.M. Torell*

The term "weed" does not always indicate that a plant is totally undesirable, or that it cannot be beneficial under certain situations. According to the above definition, many desirable species might sometimes be considered weedy; for example, a species providing valuable wildlife forage or wildlife habitat on one tract of land may be considered undesirable on land managed to maximize grass production for livestock. It all depends on the management objectives. Some plants poisonous to livestock are considered desirable ornamental plants. Other species that are almost always considered undesirable may actually provide limited benefit as they rapidly invade disturbed sites and thereby reduce soil erosion.

Some weeds in this publication are not present in all western states; however, their potential for invasion and establishment warrants concern. New weeds in your area should always be identified to determine what properties they might have that could cause future management problems. In certain instances an eradication effort should be planned to eliminate certain weed problems or prevent them from spreading. Those weeds designated as noxious in your state should be reported to the extension agent or weed control supervisor in your county unless they are already widely distributed.

To promote standardization of common plant names, this publication used the Weed Science Society of America's list of common and scientific names where available. This book has been arranged alphabetically by scientific family names with species within families arranged alphabetically by scientific name.

Because of frequently changing weed control recommendations, none have been given in this publication. For current control practices, contact your county extension agent or weed and pest supervisor.

Acknowledgments

We would like to express sincere appreciation to the authors of *Gilkey's Weeds of the Pacific Northwest*, *Weeds and Poisonous Plants of Wyoming and Utah*, and *A Guide to Selected Weeds of Oregon* for permission to duplicate slides and text from their publications. We also appreciate the help contributed by Dan Kidder who developed a listing of weeds to be used in this publication.

Appreciation is also extended to the University of Wyoming Division of Communication Services for their assistance in the layout of this publication: Elizabeth Ono Rahel, graphic design and typesetting, Allory Deiss, computer expertise, Carol Hale Stevens, graphic design and typesetting.

Great Plains yucca
Yucca glauca Nutt.

Great Plains yucca
Agavaceae
(Agave family)

Great Plains yucca is a perennial, 1 to 4 feet tall, and bush-like. It reproduces by seed and underground stems. Leaves are pale green 1 to 3 feet long, 1/4 to 1/2 inch wide, very stiff and sharply pointed, originating from the crown at ground level; flowers are large, greenish to creamy white, borne as a terminal cluster on a central stalk 1 to 4 feet tall; numerous seeds, black, flat, winged, 1/2 inch wide, are produced in an oblong fruit 2 to 3 inches long and about 1 inch thick.

Yucca is found throughout the West, mainly on dry sandy plains and prairies. Young plants and flowers are sometimes eaten by livestock. American Indians used the leaves to make baskets and the roots to produce soap. Pollination of yucca depends on a small insect, the yucca moth. The relationship between moth and plant is unique in that neither can complete its life cycle without the other.

Young plant's leaves end in a sharp spine and have thread-like fibers at their base.

Large white or green flowers are borne along a central stalk that can be four feet tall.

3

Khakiweed
Alternanthera pungens H.B.K.

Khakiweed
Amaranthaceae
(Pigweed family)

Khakiweed is a perennial with prostrate stems and thick woody vertical roots. Stems are branched, rooting at the nodes, prostrate, forming mats 1/2 to 2 feet in diameter. The plant is covered with jointed distinct hairs, especially at the stem nodes and on the back of the sepals. Leaves are opposite, oval, glassy, 1/2 to 1 1/2 inches long, may appear hairless, but usually have scattered hairs, particularly on the stalk, and those leaves of the same pair are often unequal in size. Flowers, small and whitish, are found in dense clusters around the stem at the leaf axils. Seeds are light reddish brown and shiny.

This plant, a native of tropical America, has become a serious pest in warm season turf in the Southwest.

Synonym: *Alternanthera repens* (L.) Kuntze. Non-standard name: creeping chaffweed.

Flowers are white, small and form in dense clusters in the leaf axils.

The prostrate growing habit and ability to root at the nodes coupled with a thick cuticular surface contributes to the persistent nature of this plant.

5

Tumble pigweed
Amaranthus albus L.

Tumble pigweed
Amaranthaceae
(Pigweed family)

An annual species, somewhat prostrate to spherical and erect, much branched, 6 to 36 inches tall. Leaves usually have narrower blades and shorter stalks than those of prostrate pigweed. Stems are usually light green rather than red, more erect, more intricately branched, and the general aspect of mature plants is more spiny than prostrate pigweed. Flowers are borne in small spiny clusters at the base of leaves, not in long terminal spikes as in the case of redroot pigweed. Seeds are black, shiny, lens-shaped and 0.7 to 0.8 millimeters wide.

Tumble pigweed is found primarily in cultivated or disturbed sites. This plant is a prolific seed producer and the seed can be spread great distances when mature wind-blown plants break off and tumble along the ground.

Fruit are borne in leaf axils rather than on branch terminals.

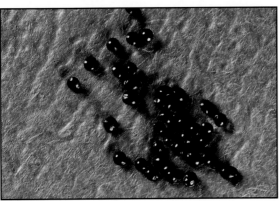

Seed of all pigweeds are shiny black.

Prostrate pigweed
Amaranthus blitoides S. Wats.

Prostrate pigweed
Amaranthaceae
(Pigweed family)

An annual with generally prostrate stems radiating in all directions from a central taproot. Main stems are usually 12 to 18 inches long with shorter secondary branches. All stems are somewhat fleshy and pliable, nearly smooth, and usually red to purple. Leaves are approximately 1/2 inch wide and oval, with the tip broader than the base. Flowers are in small congested clusters in the leaf axils. Long terminal flower spikes are absent. Seeds are shiny, black, lens-shaped and approximately twice the width of tumble pigweed seeds.

Prostrate pigweed was possibly introduced from tropical America, adapting well to our area. It occurs mostly in disturbed or cultivated soils, and is often associated with tumble pigweed or other *Amaranthus* species. It is a common garden weed.

Leaves of prostrate pigweed are oval shaped with red or purple stems. Flowers are borne in leaf axils.

Seedling plants also have red to purple stems with oval leaves.

Palmer amaranth
Amaranthus palmeri S. Wats.

Palmer amaranth is an annual, commonly 1 to 6 feet tall. There is one thick central stem with many lateral branches. Leaves are alternate, hairless, lance-shaped or egg-shaped, 2 to 8 inches long, 1/2 to 2 1/2 inches broad, and have prominent whitish veins on the underside. Male and female flowers are found on separate plants in long leafless branching spikes at the top of the plant. The slender central inflorescence, 1/2 to 1 1/2 feet tall, is much longer than any of the lateral inflorescences.

This is one of the more aggressive pigweeds and has become common in the Southwestern region. It hybridizes with other pigweeds including redroot pigweed (*A. retroflexus* L.).

Non-standard name: carelessweed.

Staminate or male flowers are borne on long terminal inflorescences and axillary clusters which at the time of fertilization give a yellowish-white appearance to the inflorescence.

Pistillate or female flowers are borne on separate plants.

Redroot pigweed
Amaranthus retroflexus L.

Redroot pigweed
Amaranthaceae
(Pigweed family)

A coarse erect annual, usually 2 to 3 feet tall. Lower stems are often red or red-striped, with color continuing down the taproot. Leaves have long petioles and prominent veins. They are somewhat broad and lance-shaped, and often become reddish. Individual flowers are small, green and tightly arranged in large, branched, spike-like, terminal clusters. Smaller axillary flower clusters may also occur. Flower clusters are full of stiff, spine-like scales, making this pigweed additionally undesirable in hay. Seeds are small, black and shiny.

Redroot pigweed is widely distributed throughout the western states, commonly found in cultivated lands, gardens, and waste areas. Germination occurs anytime during the growing season when soil moisture is sufficient. A related species, Powell amaranth (*A. powellii* S. Wats.), can be distinguished by examining the bracts, Powell amaranth having longer, narrower, pointed bracts than redroot pigweed.

Seedlings of redroot pigweed have distinct leaf veins with long petioles.

The long spiny bracts of Powell amaranth flowers distinguishes this plant from redroot pigweed.

13

Poison-ivy
Toxicodendron radicans (L.) Ktze.

Poison-ivy
Anacardiaceae
(Cashew family)

Poison-ivy is a perennial sub-shrub often less than 3 feet tall, to a distinct shrub up to 9 feet tall. Stems are simple or sparsely branched, arising from much branched subterranean stolons. Aerial roots are absent, plants never climb. Leaves alternate, compound usually with 3 leaflets. Flowers grow in axillary panicles or racemes, with five sepals united at the base and five greenish petals. Three-parted stigmas turn black with age. Fruit is globose, cream to yellow, 1/4 inch broad, wrinkled at maturity and glabrous.

The more common species west of the Cascade Mountain Range in Washington, Oregon and California is poison-oak (*T. diversilobum* (Torr. & Gray) Greene). Poison-oak is often viny, and its lateral leaflets lack stalks. These species occupy many habitats, including floodplains, river terraces, rights-of-way and other disturbed sites. The poison in these species is a milky oil found in the phloem. If the oil or its dried residue come in contact with the skin, many people develop a severe skin rash within a few hours.

Pacific poison-oak has leaves that are serrated along the margins, and are often purplish. Both poison-oak and poison-ivy usually have three leaflets per leaf, an important identification characteristic of this perennial.

Ridged fruit resembling tiny green pumpkins are formed on this poisonous species in late summer.

15

Bur chervil

Anthriscus caucalis Bieb.

Bur chervil
Apiaceae
(Parsley family)

An annual up to 3 feet tall with stems that are somewhat branched. The leaves are alternate, finely divided with a lacy appearance and generally hairy when young. Flowers are white, small and borne in few-flowered compound umbels. Fruit is about 1/8 inch long, covered by minute hooked bristles and splits into 2 one-seeded units at maturity. Plants are aromatic.

Bur chervil was introduced from Europe where it was cultivated as a garden herb. It is found along stream banks and in moist, open places, sometimes in abundance near old buildings and in farmyards.

Synonyms include: *Anthriscus scandicina* (Weber) Mansf. Non-standard name: bur beakchervil.

Compound, lacy leaves.

Small greenish flowers borne in clusters in the leaf axils and fruits are longitudinally channeled.

Wild caraway
Carum carvi L.

Wild caraway
Apiaceae
(Parsley family)

This biennial, or occasional perennial, has one or more shoots emerging from a single taproot the second year. Shoots are slender, erect, branching, furrowed, normally hollow and 1 to 3 feet tall. Leaves are alternate on shoots and oblong or oval in outline; upper leaves are long and slender with a lacy appearance; they are finely divided into linear or thread-like segments. Lower leaves appear similar, but are coarser. Flowers are small, white or pinkish, and occur in terminal or lateral, loose umbels, supported by 1/8 to 1/2 inch long pedicles. Seeds are narrow, oblong, more or less curved, 1/8 inch or more long, and brown with five conspicuous tan, linear ribs.

Wild caraway was introduced into the United States as a cultivated species, but escaped to become a weed in mountain meadows, hayfields, and along irrigation ditches and roadways in these areas. The first year's growth is a leafy rosette.

Leaves are finely divided the first year having a lacy appearance.

The inflorescence contains many white flowers and appear to be flat across the top. Seeds are oblong.

Western waterhemlock
Cicuta douglasii (DC.) Coult. & Rose

Western waterhemlock
Apiaceae
(Parsley family)

This perennial is native to the intermountain region and is highly poisonous. Erect stems are 3 to 7 feet tall, usually swollen at the base. Leaves alternate, one per node, petioled, pinnately divided. Leaf veins which terminate at the bottom of leaf serrations distinguish this species from others in the family. Flowers are white in compound stemmed umbels mostly flat on top. Each flower is two-seeded. Seeds are somewhat kidney-shaped with corky ridges and tea-colored. A horizontally-divided, enlarged taproot is its most easily-recognized feature. Juice in the taproot is extremely poisonous to animals and humans.

Western waterhemlock is a wetland plant especially common on pastures or untilled areas. It occurs along streams and irrigation canals. It begins growth in spring, flowers in late spring to early summer. Waterhemlock, considered one of the most poisonous plants in North America, is often mistaken for water-parsnip or other edible members of this family. Several deaths have occurred because of this species.

Toothed, pinnately-divided alternate leaves with veins terminating in the bottom of serrations are useful in identifying this extremely poisonous species.

When roots are split, horizontal chambers are found in western waterhemlock. This area is the most poisonous part of the plant. Extreme care should be taken when examining this species.

21

Poison hemlock
Conium maculatum L.

Poison hemlock
Apiaceae
(Parsley family)

Poison hemlock is a biennial native to Europe that grows 6 to 8 feet tall with occasional plants growing to 10 feet tall. Stems are erect, stout and purple-spotted with distinct ridges and extensively branched. Leaves are shiny green, finely pinnately divided three or four times and leaflets are segmented and 1/8 to 1/4 inch long. Lower leaves on long stalks clasp the stem; upper leaves on short stalks. Foliage has strong musty odor. Flowers are borne in many umbrella-shaped clusters, each supported by a stalk. Flowers are white with sepals lacking. Paired seeds, 1/8 inch long, are light brown, ribbed and concave.

It occurs on borders of pastures and cropland, gradually invading perennial crops (i.e. alfalfa). Poison hemlock tolerates poorly-drained soils and frequents stream and ditch banks. All plant parts are poisonous including the large white taproot. Humans have been poisoned by mistaking the plant for parsley.

Stems of poison hemlock are covered with purple spots at all growth stages.

Leaves on mature plants, as well as seedling plants (shown here), are fern-like in appearance because they are divided three and sometimes four times.

23

Wild carrot
Daucus carota L.

Wild carrot
Apiaceae
(Parsley family)

This biennial herb stands 2 to 4 feet tall. It exists as a rosette with a deep taproot the first year. Stems are erect, hollow, stiff-haired and sometimes branched. Leaves are alternate, stalked near the stem base, sessile above. Twice-pinnately compound leaves have narrow segments to 5 inches long. Leaf margins and veins have short hairs. Strong carrot odor. White flowers grow in flat-topped umbels 3 to 6 inches across with five petals. Seeds 1/8 inch long, grayish-brown, one side flattened and rounded side distinctly ribbed. Mature seeds have barbed prickles.

Wild carrot is a pernicious weed of older pastures and meadows, strongly discouraged by cultivation. Wild carrot has a strong carrot odor, and begins growth in early spring, frequents dry areas and rocky soils.

Umbels, which often close as fruits develop, are subtended by numerous prominent branching finger-like bracts.

Wild carrot has flat-topped umbel inflorescences, similar to poison hemlock and western waterhemlock.

Cow parsnip
Heracleum lanatum Michx.

Cow parsnip
Apiaceae
(Parsley family)

This native perennial reproduces by seed, forming a low-growing rosette, with a large, fleshy taproot its first year. Flower stalks grow 2 to 8 feet tall. Stems are somewhat hairy and grooved. Leaves are hairy to nearly glabrous, with serrated edges, not carrot-like. Cream colored flowers with five petals in umbels at the top of short stalks. Flower clusters are mostly flattened with outside flower stalks curving inward with maturity. Seed is flattened on one side, rounded on the other, with distinct ridges.

Cow parsnip occurs mostly in disturbed areas and along roadways. It now inhabits many sites in mountainous regions.

Leaves, commonly 6 to 10 inches across, are deeply divided, not pinnately compound like other parsley family plants.

Cow parsnip has a flat-topped umbel inflorescence.

Spreading dogbane
Apocynum androsaemifolium L.

Spreading dogbane
Apocynaceae
(Dogbane family)

Rhizomatous perennial with much-branched stems and 3/4 to 2+ feet in height. The plants exude a milky juice. Leaves are 1 to 2 3/4 inches in length, dark green above, paler beneath. Leaves are very short-stalked, spreading or drooping, with leaf blades that are rounded at the base and narrower at the apex. Flowers are pink, bell-shaped, about 1/3 to 1 inch long and borne in loose clusters at the ends of the branches and in axils of upper leaves. The fruits, two from each flower, are 2 to 5+ inches long and narrow, each fruit splits longitudinally at maturity. Seeds are numerous, small, each tipped by a tuft of white or tan hairs.

Spreading dogbane is a native species found throughout much of Canada and the U.S., with the exception of the southeastern states. It grows along roadsides, in waste areas and in orchards, and the milky juice can be toxic to livestock.

Non-standard names: flytrap dogbane and bitterroot.

Short-stalked, opposite leaves.

Loose open cluster of flowers with petal tips turned back.

29

Hemp dogbane
Apocynum cannabinum L.

Hemp dogbane
Apocynaceae
(Dogbane family)

A perennial herb reproducing by seed or rhizomes. Plants may grow up to 6 feet tall. Leaves are opposite or whorled, noticeably petioled, and somewhat ascending on opposite-branching stems. Stems often are red and exude a white milky sap when cut. Flowers are small, white to greenish-white, and arranged in clusters. Fruiting structures are long pendulous follicles, 5 inches or more in length, which usually turn reddish brown at maturity.

Hemp dogbane is a widespread native species that can become weedy along roadsides, waste areas, and on non-cultivated agricultural lands. It has been called Indian hemp, because of its use as a source of high-quality fiber by pre-historic tribes. Several other similar-appearing dogbane species are common to the western United States, including spreading dogbane (*A. androsaemifolium* L.) and prairie dogbane (*A. sibiricum* Jacq.). Flower size is a key characteristic in distinguishing between the various dogbanes. Hybridization between species is reportedly frequent in this genus. Hemp dogbane, spreading dogbane, and possibly others of this genus are poisonous to livestock.

Non-standard name: common dogbane.

Most leaves are erect or ascending, and have a short but distinct petiole. Stems are often dark red.

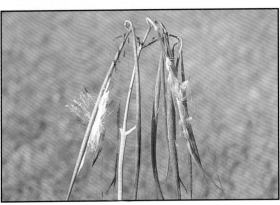

Mature hanging follicles are 5 inches long or more, and contain slender tufted seeds.

31

Mexican whorled milkweed
Asclepias fascicularis Dcne.

Mexican whorled milkweed
Asclepiadaceae
(Milkweed family)

Mexican whorled milkweed is an erect perennial 2 to 4 feet tall spreading by creeping underground roots. Stems are smooth to minutely pubescent. Leaves are linear to lance-shaped, 1 1/2 to 4 1/2 inches long, 1/4 to 1/2 inch wide, short-petioled, found in whorls of 3 to 6, and are commonly folded along the midrib. Flowers, borne in umbels found in the upper leaf axils, are white to greenish or purple-tinted. Fruit is a follicle which is erect, 2 to 4 1/2 inches long, smooth, narrow, and ends in a point. Seeds are about 1/4 inch long and have a tuft of hair attached.

This plant, which may be confused with the western and eastern whorled milkweed (*A. subverticillata* (Gray) Vail and *A. verticillata* L., respectively), except for the wider leaves, is a native of western America, perhaps first known in Mexico. This plant, like the other milkweeds tested, is also toxic to livestock.

Non-standard name: narrowleaf milkweed.

Showy flowers are borne in umbels at the top of the plant.

The flowering structure is a long, narrow follicle, which contains small brown seeds.

Swamp milkweed
Asclepias incarnata L.

Swamp milkweed
Asclepiadaceae
(Milkweed family)

A herbaceous perennial, spreading from short rootstocks or seed. Plants are erect, growing 3 to 4 feet tall. Leaves are opposite, mostly smooth, lance-shaped, and have a short petiole. Flowers are pink to rose-purple, arranged in clusters at the tops of plants. Tufted seeds are produced in clusters of smooth erect pods (follicles). Individual pods are 2 1/2 to 3 1/2 inches long. Plants exude a thin milky juice when injured.

Swamp milkweed is poisonous and is suspected of causing livestock deaths. It is found in low wet meadows, marshes, and along streams and ditchbanks.

Pink flowers form in terminal clusters.

Seeds are produced in slender erect pods.

35

Labriform milkweed
Asclepias labriformis Jones

Labriform milkweed
Asclepiadaceae
(Milkweed family)

A herbaceous perennial with milky juice, spreading by seed and from roots. Plants are erect, with mostly non-branching stems, 10 to 24 inches tall. Smooth pale green leaves are 2 to 6 inches long and 1/4 to 1 inch wide. Basal leaves are opposite; while upper leaves are alternate. Pale yellowish green flowers are arranged in umbrella-like clusters. Fruits are hanging egg-shaped to long, narrow follicles, 1 1/2 to 3 inches long and 1/2 to 1 1/4 inches wide. Seeds are flat, each bearing a tuft of long silky hairs.

Labriform milkweed is a native species considered to be the most poisonous of all western milkweeds. As little as one ounce of green leaf material from this species can kill an adult sheep. It is found primarily in mixed desert shrub communities on sandy sites in southeastern Utah, northern Arizona, and western Colorado.

Non-standard name: Jones milkweed.

Close-up of pale yellowish-green labriform milkweed flowers.

Fruits are egg-shaped follicles with seeds containing a papus.

37

Showy milkweed
Asclepias speciosa Torr.

Showy Milkweed
Asclepiadaceae
(Milkweed family)

Showy milkweed is perennial, 2 to 5 feet tall, reproducing by seeds and underground rootstocks. Leaves are opposite, oval-shaped, prominently veined, 4 to 7 inches long, and covered with fine, soft hairs. The plant has a grayish-green color and grows erect. All foliage parts exude a milky latex sap when cut. Flowers are arranged in umbels at the top of the plant and are purplish-pink. Reddish-brown flat seeds are borne in 3 to 5 inch long, narrow pods. Each seed bears a tuft of hairs allowing them to be spread by wind.

Common milkweed (*A. syriaca* L.) is found on the eastern slope of the Rocky Mountains. Showy milkweed is native to North America and is common along roadsides, ditchbanks, pastures and cultivated fields. Colonies form by spreading rootstocks when the plant is not disturbed by tillage practices.

Seed pods, 3 to 5 inches long, burst open in late summer, producing dozens of flat, reddish-brown seeds. Fibers produced within seed capsules are used commercially.

Clustered flowers, purplish-pink in color, appear in mid-summer on showy milkweed.

39

Western whorled milkweed
Asclepias subverticillata (Gray) Vail

Western whorled milkweed
Asclepiadaceae
(Milkweed family)

An erect hairless perennial reproducing by seed and deep rooted horizontal roots. Stems, slender, 1 to 3 feet tall, smooth, erect, and unbranched, arise from a branched rootcrown either singly or in clumps. Leaves, narrow, up to 3/8 inch wide and 2 to 5 inches long, occur in whorls, mostly three or four per node and are nearly stalkless with secondary clusters of small leaves in at least some of the axils. Flowers are green-white, found in umbrella-like clusters at the top of the branches and in leaf axils. The erect follicles (seedpods), 2 to 4 inches long, narrow and long pointed, contain many flat brown seeds which have a tuft of silky hair at the top.

This plant, which is native in the western United States and Mexico, is very similar to eastern whorled milkweed (*A. verticillata* L.), which is more common in other regions of the U.S., and can be distinguished by floral characteristics and with very few small leaf branches in leaf axils. Both species are toxic, though not palatable, with western whorled milkweed being more toxic.

Non-standard names: horsetail milkweed, poison milkweed, whorled milkweed.

Flowers are borne in umbrella-like structures at the top of the plant. Leaves are arranged in whorls.

Seeds have a white tuft of hairs which aids in their dispersal.

Western yarrow
Achillea lanulosa Nutt.

Western yarrow
Asteraceae
(Sunflower family)

This is an aromatic perennial with stems, 1 to 2 feet tall, with woolly hairs, arising singly or loosely clustered from a weakly spreading root system. Leaves equally distributed along the stem; blade lanceolate in outline but finely dissected into many ultimate segments, overall dimensions are 2 to 6 inches long and 1/4 to 1 inch wide. Inflorescence with many small heads in a flat-topped or dome-shaped cluster with five white or pink ray flowers, and 10 to 20 disk flowers.

This species includes a complex of several ill-defined phases and polyploid races. It is widely distributed throughout the temperate northern hemisphere. Though seldom a weed problem, it is widespread, occupying many plant communities including aspen, conifer, sagebrush, mountain brush, riparian, meadow and alpine at 4,000 to 11,000 feet. The flowering period is June to August. Its elimination should only be on private land after careful evaluation.

Western yarrow is most commonly found in the U.S. while common yarrow (*Achillea millefolium* L.) is a Eurasian species.

Leaves are finely divided and appear feather-like.

Flower heads are clustered having a flat-topped appearance.

Annual bursage
Ambrosia acanthicarpa Hook.

Annual bursage
Asteraceae
(Sunflower family)

This branching annual, 1 to 3 feet tall, may have long to short hairs, or both. Leaves are more or less lobed, opposite below, having petioles, alternate above, the uppermost becoming sessile. Flowers on the same plant are male and female, at different locations. Male flowers in terminal inflorescences with the heads stalked and drooping. Female flowers are spiny.

This species resembles common ragweed (*A. artemisiifolia* L.), with annual bursage being more conspicuously stiff-haired, particularly on young leaves. The fruit is covered by several circles of sharp spines. It also resembles slimleaf bursage (*A. confertiflora* DC.), except slimleaf bursage is a perennial bush with creeping rootstalks. Annual bursage has fruits which are beak-tipped, granular, armed with 10 to 20 curved spines ending in a definite hook.

Abundant in both crop and noncrop areas, this native plant can be found in various soil types.

Seedling stage show distinct hairs on the leaf surface.

Staminate heads are borne in a terminal inflorescence whereas the pistillate flowers, having distinct spines are borne in leaf axils.

Common ragweed
Ambrosia artemisiifolia L.

Common ragweed
Asteraceae
(Sunflower family)

This native annual reaches 4 feet tall. Stems and leaves are blue-green and are covered with fine hairs. Leaves are pinnately divided and are both alternate and opposite. The bottom side of the leaf has a gray appearance because of fine hairs. Flowers are found on terminal branches, which have male and female flowers in clusters with staminate flowers found above the pistillate flowers. Seeds are awl-shaped with a spiny projection on one side. Flowering occurs in late summer, with seeds maturing by October.

This annual is common throughout the western U.S. causing many individuals to have hay fever. Even though it is common, it is not highly competitive in crops or rangeland. It is commonly found along ditches and in waste areas. Western ragweed (*A. psilostachya* DC.) is shorter in stature and is commonly found on rangeland and perennial cropland.

Seedlings appear in early spring for this annual weed. Leaves are deeply-lobed with rounded tips.

Numerous flowers appear in early fall on terminal stems. Pollen is produced at that time, causing many people to have hay fever.

Woollyleaf bursage
Ambrosia grayi (A.Nels.) Shinners

Woollyleaf bursage
Asteraceae
(Sunflower family)

An aggressive creeping perennial, 1 to 2 feet tall, covered with silver-gray pubescence, reproducing by seed borne in leaf axils, but principally by extensive rootstalks, forming large clonal populations. Leaves alternate, narrowed at the base to a distinct petiole, sometimes with several small lobes. Leaf blade ovate to lanceolate in outline, up to 3 inches long and 2 1/2 inches wide. Male and female flowers are found in separate locations on the plant. Male inflorescence is stalked and elongated or spike-like. Female flowers are found in clusters or singular in the axils of the upper leaves.

Woollyleaf bursage is a native plant found in the central and southern Great Plains region. In the past this plant has often been confused with skeleton-leaf bursage *(Ambrosia tomentosa* (Nutt.) A. Nels.), which has leaves that are more deeply lobed.

Newly emerging woollyleaf bursage plants are deeply lobed.

As plants mature, leaves appear gray-green because of their fine dense hairs.

Skeletonleaf bursage
Ambrosia tomentosa Nutt.

Skeletonleaf bursage
Asteraceae
(Sunflower family)

Skeletonleaf bursage is a perennial 4 to 18 inches tall with extensive creeping rootstocks. Stems are branched and somewhat spreading; leaves 2 to 5 inches long alternate, ovate to lanceolate in outline, coarsely toothed and deeply segmented with the lower surface covered with minute white hairs. The upper surface is smooth and green. Flowers are inconspicuous and yellow. Staminate flowers are found in solitary, elongated, terminal clusters; pistillate flowers form in pairs in leaf axils below. Fruit is a light brown bur with conical spines and contains one or more achenes.

This weed is a native of the plains region. It grows in cultivated fields, pastures, prairies and waste areas. It also survives well under varied soil moisture conditions. Skeletonleaf bursage is a difficult weed to eradicate because of its extensive horizontal root system. Flowering and seed production occur from late June to August.

Leaves are deeply lobed with a dark green upper surface and a silvery-green lower surface which is covered with fine hairs.

Terminal flower clusters with inconspicuous yellow flowers appear in late summer.

51

Giant ragweed
Ambrosia trifida L.

Giant ragweed
Asteraceae
(Sunflower family)

Giant ragweed, a native annual exceeding 10 feet in height in moist locations, can mature as smaller plants in drier areas. Stems and leaves are rough, leaves are palmately divided, normally having three lobes. Leaves can also have up to five lobes or be unlobed. Leaves are opposite with long petioles attached to a single center stem. Flowers are located in terminal clusters and are male (staminate) and female (pistillate). Seeds are over 1/4 inch in length with four or five terminal spikes on each.

Giant ragweed is common in the western U.S., often found in moist areas, near roadsides and in wasteland. A major cause of hay fever in the United States. It is not a highly competitive species in crop or rangeland and can be controlled at early growth stages with herbicides.

Large, deeply-parted leaves are normally lobed three times, but may contain up to five lobes.

Flower clusters, often over 6 inches long, appear in the fall. Pollen shed at that time causes people to have hay fever problems.

53

Mayweed chamomile
Anthemis cotula L.

Mayweed chamomile
Asteraceae
(Sunflower family)

Mayweed chamomile is an annual bushy, branched plant that is ill-smelling. Plants are from 1/2 to 2 feet tall with leaves several times divided into narrow segments. Flowers 3/4 inch in diameter, usually having 12 white ray flowers, are borne at ends of branches and in leaf axils. Flowering occurs from May to October.

Corn chamomile (*Anthemis arvensis* L.) looks almost identical but is easily identified because of its lack of odor.

Mayweed is a European native which now occurs worldwide. It is of no value but common throughout the Pacific Northwest and California. It can adapt to many different growing conditions and is commonly found in waste areas, barnyards, cultivated fields and overgrazed pastures. Contact with mayweed can cause skin rashes, blistering of livestock muzzles, and irritation to mucous membranes of grazing livestock. It can impart a strong flavor to the milk of dairy animals.

Non-standard name: dog fennel.

Leaves having a foul odor, are divided several times into narrow segments.

Flowers bloom from May to October and are 3/4 inch in diameter.

Common burdock
Arctium minus (Hill) Bernh.

Common burdock
Asteraceae
(Sunflower family)

Common burdock is a biennial, producing a rosette of large, cordate, thickly hairy leaves the first year and an erect, much branched, coarse stem 3 to 10 feet tall the second year. The leaves are alternate, large, broadest at the leaf base, somewhat diminished upwards, margins toothed or wavy, woolly beneath at least when young, dark green above. Flowers are purple, heads borne in leaf axils or at the end of branches, numerous, clustered, covered with many slender, hooked spines, achenes gray to brown, mottled, oblong, about 1/4 inch long, flattened and slightly curved.

Native of Europe, common burdock is now established throughout much of the U.S. It is commonly found growing along roadsides, ditchbanks, in pastures and waste areas. The burs can become entangled in the hair of livestock allowing seed to be distributed to new areas. Flowering and seed production occur from July to September.

The first year common burdock produces large leaves with no flowers.

Purple flowers are borne in bur-like structures from mid-summer until fall. Spines hooked on the end gave rise to the idea for Velcro.

Biennial wormwood
Artemisia biennis Willd.

Biennial wormwood
Asteraceae
(Sunflower family)

Biennial wormwood is a nonaromatic annual or biennial growing up to 6 feet tall. Leaves are oval and often toothed, 2 to 5 inches long. Inflorescence is a series of spike-like glabrous clusters. Stems arise from a taproot and often branch from the base. Stems are often reddish and greater than 1/2 inch in diameter. Flowering occurs from September to October. Absinth wormwood (*A. absinthium*), a perennial, grows 16 to 48 inches tall with relatively large dissected leaves which are 1 1/4 to 3 inches long.

Biennial wormwood is thought to be a native of the northwest U.S. but is common in the Great Plains from Colorado northward. It is frequently found near streams, lakes or irrigation ditches.

Absinth wormwood is a robust plant with relatively large leaves which are oblong in shape.

The first year following biennial wormwood germination a rosette having slender divided leaves may or may not flower.

Common sagewort

Artemisia campestris L.

Common sagewort
Asteraceae
(Sunflower family)

Common sagewort is a biennial forming a rosette the first year then a seed head the second. Leaves are long with petioles and sometimes divided into 3 thread-like segments. Plants produce seed stalks up to 3 feet long. Upright stems are covered with leafy branches on their upper half. Flowers located on short stalks are erect, nodding when mature in August and September. Seeds mature in October.

This biennial plant is common throughout pastures and rangeland and is often found along ditches and near roads. It is not considered a highly competitive plant.

The first year's growth of common sagewort is blue-green with leaves that are deeply lobed.

Flowers borne along stems mature in August and September.

Silver sagebrush
Artemisia cana Pursh

Silver sagebrush
Asteraceae
(Sunflower family)

Silver sagebrush is a native perennial capable of reproducing by seeds and resprouting from roots when topgrowth is destroyed. Leaves are simple, alternate and lance shaped, occasionally with 1 or 2 irregular teeth. Leaves are covered with fine hair giving them a silver color. Flowers appear in August and September within leafy panicles. Seeds have 4 or 5 ribs and are shed in October to December. Yellowish stems reach heights of over 6 feet when plants mature.

Plants are highly competitive with perennial grasses. They generally increase with cattle usage and decrease in population with sheep usage. Plants are used as browse for wildlife and sheep. Habitats include loamy and sandy soils. Control measures such as herbicides and fire are only partially effective because of the resprouting nature of this woody species.

Leaves, covered with hair, are simple, alternate and lance-shaped ending in a single point.

Yellow flowers form in late summer along the stems of silver sagebrush.

Sand sagebrush
Artemisia filifolia Torr.

Sand sagebrush
Asteraceae
(Sunflower family)

Sand sagebrush, a perennial, grows to heights of 3 feet and reproduces from seed. Stems are fine in nature, woody and branched, having a gray appearance from pubescence on leaves and stems. Leaves are threadlike, 1 1/2 to 3 inches long. Fruit are borne in upper leaf axils as rounded structures. Flowers form a plume-like structure from July to October, with seeds maturing in October.

Sand sagebrush grows on sandy, well-drained soils in rangeland and pastures.

Leaves of this perennial woody, species are thread-like, growing from 1 1/2 to 3 inches in length.

Seedling plants of sand sagebrush have thread-like leaves.

Fringed sagebrush
Artemisia frigida Willd.

Fringed sagebrush
Asteraceae
(Sunflower family)

Fringed sagebrush is a perennial reproducing by seeds. Plants reach heights of 1 1/2 feet. Plants are mat-like with a silvery color before producing flower stalks. The plant has a strong sagebrush odor, is silvery blue and is bitter to taste. Leaves are finely divided into either 3 or 5 segments up to 1 1/2 inches long. Flowers are yellow, and are borne within long hairy bracts. Achene or oblong seed are flattened with rounded edges and are gray to brown. Flowering begins in August with seeds maturing in September.

Fringed sagebrush is an important wildlife and sheep feed source, but is highly competitive with perennial grasses needed by cattle. It is widespread on rangeland and increases rapidly with overgrazing. Herbicides are effective in controlling this species.

Early spring growth of fringed sagebrush appears as blue-green clusters within a gray background.

Fringed sagebrush, a mat-forming plant, produces seed stalks in late summer and fall with round yellow flower heads and hairy bracts.

Big sagebrush
Artemisia tridentata Nutt.

Big sagebrush
Asteraceae
(Sunflower family)

Big sagebrush is a perennial reproducing from seed. Plants average less than 3 feet in height; but in deep soils this woody species reaches heights over 10 feet. It is considered an evergreen even though leaves have a grayer color in winter months. Leaves are undivided, wedge-shaped with 3 blunt lobes. Leaves contain oils causing them to have a distinct odor when crushed. They are silvery blue because of the dense gray hairs found on both sides. Yellow flowers appear in late August, forming panicles. Seed formation and shed takes place from October to December. Seed have a one-year viability once they are shed. Older plants have trunks over 3 inches in diameter, which are covered with brown stringy bark.

Big sagebrush is a highly competitive species and often limits perennial grass production to 1/3 that of areas which have been cleared of sagebrush. It is the most common woody species in western U.S. rangelands. Control cannot be obtained by grazing management alone. Excellent control has been attained for over 20 years by treating with herbicides, burning or mechanical removal of the species.

This woody perennial has blue-green strap-shaped leaves with 3 distinct lobes at the tips.

Flowers are formed in August with seed being shed from September to December.

69

English daisy
Bellis perennis L.

English daisy
Asteraceae
(Sunflower family)

A perennial with basal leaves with a prostrate or spreading growth habit. Leaves are nearly smooth or loosely hairy, entire margined or toothed, broad above, narrowed at the base to a long stalk. Flower heads, erect and long-stalked, are white or pinkish with yellow centers. The stalks generally exceed the leaves in length.

English daisy was introduced from Europe as a garden plant. It is well known across the northern U.S. as a lawn weed.

Non-standard names: European daisy and lawn daisy.

Flower, borne on long stalks, have white petals with yellow centers.

Prostrate growth habit is well adapted to turf environments.

Nodding beggarticks
Bidens cernua L.

Nodding beggarticks
Asteraceae
(Sunflower family)

Annual; stem branching, erect stems up to 4 feet tall, nearly smooth; leaves without stalks, undivided, toothed; heads with yellow flowers, nodding; fruit generally with 4 horns.

Devils beggarticks (*B. frondosa* L.) is similar except leaves are long-stalked and divided into 3 or 5 sharply toothed leaflets; heads do not nod, fruits have 2 horns.

Found frequently on moist soils in low areas and waste places; not found in cultivated fields. Several other species similar to these are found in the region.

Non-standard names: bur marigold or sticktight.

The leaves of devils beggarticks are stalked and the flowers are not nodding.

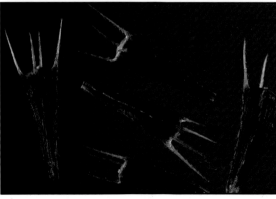

Note the 4 horns on the fruit of nodding beggarticks; there are only 2 on devils beggarticks.

Plumeless thistle
Carduus acanthoides L.

Plumeless thistle
Asteraceae
(Sunflower family)

Plumeless thistle is a winter annual or biennial herb, from a stout fleshy tap-root, rarely flowering the first year. Stems grow from 1 to 4 feet tall; they are freely branched above and covered with spiny wings 1/4 to 3/4 inch wide extending up to the flowering heads. Basal rosette leaves are usually 4 to 8 inches long with spinose lobes. Stem leaves alternate, sessile and blending into the stem. Peduncles usually spiny-winged up to the base of the flowering heads; heads solitary at the ends of branches or in clusters of 2 to 5. Involucral bracts narrowly lanceolate, sparsely to densely hairy. Corolla mostly purple, rarely white or yellowish.

This native of Eurasia is infrequent to locally abundant in pastures, stream valleys, fields and roadsides. It is frequently found in Idaho, Colorado and Wyoming and has the potential of becoming a widespread noxious weed. Flowering occurs from May to July.

A seedling rosette of plumeless thistle has wavy leaves with yellow spines along the leaf margins.

Flower heads, 1 to 2 inches in diameter, are purplish-pink with bracts holding the seed appearing as sharp spines. Flowering occurs from May to July.

Musk thistle
Carduus nutans L.

Musk thistle
Asteraceae
(Sunflower family)

Musk thistle is biennial or sometimes a winter annual, which grows up to 6 feet tall. Leaves are dark green with light green midrib, deeply lobed, and spiny margined. Leaves extend onto the stem giving a winged appearance. Flower heads are terminal, solitary, 1 1/2 to 3 inches in diameter, and usually bent over. Flowers are deep rose, violet or purple, occasionally white; they are subtended by broad, spine-tipped bracts. Fruits are 3/16 inch long, shiny, yellowish-brown with a plume of white hair-like fibers.

Musk thistle was introduced to the U.S. in the early part of the century and is now widespread throughout the U.S. and Canada. It is native to southern Europe and western Asia. It invades pasture, range and forest lands along with roadsides, waste areas, ditch banks, stream banks and grain fields. It spreads rapidly forming extremely dense stands which crowd out desirable forages. Chemical control is effective. An introduced biological control agent, the musk thistle weevil, feeds on the seeds and can limit the spread of this plant.

Musk thistle seedlings have wavy margins and are somewhat lobed with marginal yellow spines.

Flowers appear on this biennial in mid-summer. Flower heads are deep rose and up to 3 inches wide. Bracts under the flower are a very distinctive identification feature.

Italian thistle
Carduus pycnocephalus L.

Italian thistle
Asteraceae
(Sunflower family)

Annual or sometimes biennial; stems more or less woolly, mostly 1 to 4 feet in height, with spiny wings. Leaves deeply cut into 2 to 5 pairs of lobes, terminal spine of the lobe the longest and most rigid, undersurface of leaves thinly woolly. Flowers purplish or pinkish, borne in cylindric heads, these solitary or in clusters of 2 to 5 at the ends of the branches, the bracts hairy; fruits from the outer flowers gray in color, those from the inner portion of the head yellowish to tan.

Italian thistle is native to the Mediterranean region of southern Europe. The plant flowers during May and June and is generally senescent by mid-July. Italian thistle infests roadsides and waste areas, and can be a major problem on hill pasture land.

Slenderflower thistle (*Carduus tenuiflorus* W. Curtis) closely resembles Italian thistle. Slenderflower thistle usually has more than 5 heads per cluster and the bracts are not hairy.

Non-standard name: compact-headed thistle.

The flower stalk of Italian thistle (left) has fewer heads than the slenderflowered thistle (right).

Deeply lobed leaves of an Italian thistle seedling.

79

Distaff thistle
Carthamus lanatus L.

Distaff thistle
Asteraceae
(Sunflower family)

Distaff thistle is a spiny annual having stems up to 3 1/2 feet tall. Leaves are alternate, clasping at the base, rigid, deeply toothed with long stout marginal spines, conspicuously veined, glandular and hairy, with the hairs, at least in the axils, more or less cobweb-like. Flowers, yellow with red veins, are borne in spiny heads. Fruits, about 3/16 inch long, are straw colored with some deeper brown or black, with those of the inner flowers being topped with a persistent ring of scales.

Distaff thistle, native of the Mediterranean region, has been found in the eastern region of the U.S. and occasionally in California and Oregon. The known infestations appear to be spreading. The plant is a serious threat to range and pastures, due to its spiny nature.

The spiny leaves and stems and aggressive nature make this plant a serious threat in both range and pasture situations.

Yellow flowers have spiny bracts, red veins and a cobweb-like pubescence.

Cornflower
Centaurea cyanus L.

Cornflower
Asteraceae
(Sunflower family)

An annual with stems that are simple or branched up to 3 feet tall. Leaves are narrow, generally not toothed, or the lower leaves sometimes toothed or lobed. The whole plant is at first grayish hairy. The heads are long stalked, showy, 1+ inches in diameter, blue, purple, pink, red, or white.

This Mediterranean native has spread to many parts of the world, no doubt as an ornamental species.

Non-standard name: bachelor's button.

Flower head is showy and about 1 1/2 inches in diameter.

The flowers range in color from white to red to blue to purple.

Diffuse knapweed
Centaurea diffusa Lam.

Diffuse knapweed
Asteraceae
(Sunflower family)

This weed is a diffusely branched annual or short-lived perennial, 1 to 2 feet tall, stems are rough to the touch. Leaves are pinnately divided; the reduced leaves of the inflorescence are mostly entire. Flowering heads are numerous and narrow. Flowers are white to rose or sometimes purplish; margins of involucral bracts are divided like the teeth of a comb, and bracts are tipped with a definite slender spine. Achenes are brown or grayish; pappus is lacking.

Centaurea is a large genus of over 400 species, most originating in the Mediterranean region. All of the species treated here have been introduced from Eurasia and now represent a threat to pastures and rangelands. Diffuse knapweed infests roadsides, waste areas and dry rangelands, and as a highly competitive plant, threatens to exclude many desirable species. Flowering occurs from July to September.

Seedlings of diffuse knapweed have finely divided leaves covered with short hair. Herbicides are most effective when applied at this early growth stage.

Bracts under the flowers have yellow spines with teeth appearing as a comb along the spine margins.

85

Iberian starthistle
Centaurea iberica Trev. ex Spreng.

Iberian starthistle
Asteraceae
(Sunflower family)

Iberian starthistle is annual or biennial. Plants are prolific seed producers reaching heights of over 6 feet when mature. Plants form a rosette in late May and June and flower in July and August. The stems and leaves are covered with fine hairs with leaves being divided into narrow linear segments with the leaf tip narrow and undivided. The bracts of the purple flowers have straw-colored, spinelike projections over one inch in length. Seeds are light tan and topped with a plume of short flattened bristles.

Introduced from Europe, this species was reported abundant in California in the early 1950s in some counties. It has been reported in several western U.S. states. Purple starthistle (*C. calcitrapa* L.) closely resembles Iberian starthistle. Mature seed heads are needed to distinguish between the two species. If these species are found they should be treated with a herbicide to keep them from spreading. Inform your County Extension Service or Weed Control Districts of the location of these species.

Seedlings appear in early spring. Leaves are deeply lobed with light colored midribs.

Flowers are light purple with yellow spines, over an inch long, extending from the involucre.

Spotted knapweed
Centaurea maculosa Lam.

Spotted knapweed
Asteraceae
(Sunflower family)

Spotted knapweed is a biennial or usually short-lived perennial with a stout taproot. It can have one or more stems, branched 1 to 3 feet tall. Basal leaves up to 6 inches long, blades narrowly elliptic to oblanceolate, entire to pinnately parted; principal stem leaves pinnately divided. Flowering heads are solitary at end of branches; involucral bracts stiff and tipped with a dark comblike fringe. The ray flowers are pinkish-purple or rarely cream-colored. Fruits are about 1/8 inch long, tipped with a tuft of persistent bristles.

Spotted knapweed, which was introduced from Eurasia as a contaminant of alfalfa and clover seed, ranks as the number one weed problem on rangeland in western Montana. Other western states are experiencing a reduction in desirable plant communities as this species is allowed to spread. Knapweeds readily establish themselves on any disturbed soil, and their early spring growth makes them competitive for soil moisture and nutrients. There is some evidence that knapweeds release chemical substances which inhibit surrounding vegetation. The flowering period extends from June to October.

Spotted knapweed rosettes appear in early spring as deeply lobed leaves radiating from a common point. Herbicides are most effective when applied at this growth stage.

Flowers of spotted knapweed are usually pinkish-purple. Bracts under the flowers have dark spots tipped with fringe. Leaves of the mature plant are finely divided.

89

Meadow knapweed
Centaurea pratensis Thuill.

Meadow knapweed
Asteraceae
(Sunflower family)

Perennial; up to 3 1/2 feet tall with many branches. Lower leaves long-stalked, entire, coarsely lobed, or toothed, middle and upper leaves without stalks or nearly so, entire or toothed, the uppermost leaves usually much reduced and entire. Flowers borne in large pink to purplish-red heads at the end of the branches; involucral bracts deeply fringed, light to dark brown. This species is considered to be a hybrid between brown knapweed (*Centaurea jacea* L.)and black knapweed (*Centaurea nigra* L.).

Meadow knapweed is native to Europe and is now common in British Columbia, Oregon and northern California. It infests roadsides, waste areas, fields and pastures.

Flowers larger and more spreading than some other knapweed species. Bracts below the flower are deeply lobed.

Leaf margins may be entire as shown or toothed.

Russian knapweed
Centaurea repens L.

Russian knapweed
Asteraceae
(Sunflower family)

Russian knapweed is perennial, forming dense colonies by adventitious shoots from widely spreading black roots. Stems are erect, openly branched, 18 to 36 inches tall. Lower leaves are deeply lobed, 2 to 4 inches long; upper leaves entire or serrate, narrow to a sessile base. Cone-shaped flowering heads are 1/4 to 1/2 inch in diameter, solitary at the tip of leafy branchlets. Flowers are pink to lavender. Many pearly involucral bracts form with rounded or acute papery margins.

Russian knapweed is a native of Eurasia, probably introduced in North America about 1898. It is now widely established in the western U.S. This species forms colonies in cultivated fields, orchards, pastures and roadsides. Russian knapweed plants spread by black, deep growing roots which penetrate to a depth of over 8 feet. Flowering occurs from June to September.

Leaves of newly emerging plants are toothed and covered with fine hair, giving them a blue-green color.

Flowers of this perennial are pinkish-purple. Bracts have pointed papery tips.

93

Yellow starthistle
Centaurea solstitialis L.

Yellow starthistle
Asteraceae
(Sunflower family)

Yellow starthistle is an annual, 2 to 3 feet tall, has rigid branching, winged stems covered with a cottony pubescence. Basal leaves are deeply lobed while upper leaves are entire and sharply pointed. Flower heads are yellow, located singly on ends of branches, and armed with sharp straw-colored thorns up to 3/4 inch long. Fruits from ray flowers are dark-colored without bristles, while fruits from disk flowers are lighter and have a tuft of white bristles.

Yellow starthistle, introduced from Europe, grows on various soil types and is usually introduced on roadsides and waste areas. "Chewing disease" results when horses are forced to eat the yellow starthistle.

A related species, Malta starthistle (*C. melitensis* L.) is similar to the yellow starthistle except the Malta starthistle has smaller seed heads having smaller spines which are branched at the base.

Seedling plants appear in early spring. Leaves have deeply lobed margins with pointed tips.

Yellow flowers appear on this annual plant in mid-summer. Yellow spines up to 3/4 inch long extend from the involucre or seed case.

95

Squarrose knapweed
Centaurea virgata Lam. var. *squarrosa* (Willd.) Boiss.

Squarrose knapweed
Asteraceae
(Sunflower family)

A long-lived taprooted perennial typically reaching heights of 12 to 18 inches. Stems are highly branched, with deeply dissected lower leaves and bract-like upper leaves. Flower heads are relatively small, containing 4 to 8 rose or pink colored flowers, usually developing no more than 3 to 4 seeds per head. Bract tips are recurved or spreading, with the terminal spine longer than lateral spines on each bract. It is often confused with diffuse knapweed, but differs principally in the fact that it is a true perennial, and bracts are recurved. Unlike diffuse knapweed, seed heads are highly deciduous, falling off the stems soon after seeds mature.

Squarrose knapweed is a competitive rangeland weed native to the eastern Mediterranean area. It is not yet widely distributed in the West, but has gained footholds in Utah, California and Oregon.

Flower head showing recurved bract tips.

Seedling showing deeply indented gray-green leaves.

Rush skeletonweed

Chondrilla juncea L.

Rush skeletonweed
Asteraceae
(Sunflower family)

Rush skeletonweed is a perennial, 1 to 4 feet tall. Starting at the stem base for 4 to 6 inches, stems usually have downwardly bent coarse hairs; smooth stems above. Leaves form in a basal rosette, sharply toothed, and wither as the flower stem develops. Leaves of the stem are inconspicuous, narrow and entire. Flowering heads are scattered on branches, approximately 3/4 inch in diameter, with 7 to 15 yellow, strap-shaped flowers. Seeds are pale brown to nearly black, about 1/8 inch long. Body of seed is several-ribbed, smooth below with tiny scaly projections above, terminated by a long beak with numerous soft white bristles.

Rush skeletonweed is an introduced Eurasian species which presently infests several million acres in Idaho, Oregon, Washington and California. It generally inhabits well-drained, light-textured soils along roadsides, in rangelands, grain fields and pastures. Soil disturbance aids establishment. The extensive and deep root system makes skeletonweed difficult to control. Cut surfaces of the leaves and stems exude a milky latex. Flowering and seed production occur from mid-July through frost.

Rosettes resemble those of a dandelion, but are readily distinguished when stem elongation starts in early summer when red hairs are usually present.

Yellow flowerheads, less than one inch wide, have strap-shaped petals that are flat across the end with distinct lobes or teeth.

Oxeye daisy

Chrysanthemum leucanthemum L.

Oxeye daisy
Asteraceae
(Sunflower family)

Oxeye daisy is an erect rhizomatous perennial, 10 to 24 inches tall, glabrous to sparsely hairy. Leaves progressively reduce in size upward on stem. Basal and lower stem leaves are oblanceolate to narrowly obovate, 2 to 5 inches long including the petiole, margin crenate to lobed or parted. Upper leaves become sessile and merely toothed. Flowering heads are solitary at the ends of branches, about 1 1/2 inches long. Fruits have about 10 ribs.

Oxeye daisy is a native of Eurasia and has escaped cultivation. It can be found in meadows, roadsides, and waste places. Flowering occurs from June through August.

Leaves of this creeping perennial have lobed margins with basal leaves growing up to 5 inches long.

Flower heads having white ray flowers and yellow disk flowers. This species is often transplanted as an ornamental.

101

Gray rabbitbrush
Chrysothamnus nauseosus (Pallas) Britt.

Gray rabbitbrush
Asteraceae
(Sunflower family)

This perennial is strongly scented with many branches. Stems, silky or white woolly covered, are 2 to 4 feet tall. Leaves are numerous, slender, alternate, not twisted, 3/4 to 2 inches long. Flowers are yellow, terminal in large clusters. Fruits are five-angled and hairy.

Gray rabbitbrush, also commonly called rubber rabbitbrush, is one of at least 12 native species of *Chrysothamnus* that occur mainly in the western U.S. They grow well on dry soils and are often associated with sagebrush. Gray rabbitbrush is an invader and its presence in dense stands indicates overgrazing. Plants rate low in palatability but sheep and wildlife will eat it. Indians used gray rabbitbrush as chewing gum, for yellow dye, tea, and for medicine. Control of this undesirable shrub is difficult due to its ability to resprout from the crown after being sprayed or burned.

Non-standard name: rubber rabbitbrush.

Stems of gray rabbitbrush are covered with fine hair, giving them a white color. Leaves are narrow and straight.

Yellow flowers appear in late summer on stem terminals as large clusters.

103

Douglas rabbitbrush
Chrysothamnus viscidiflorus (Hook.) Nutt.

Douglas rabbitbrush
Asteraceae
(Sunflower family)

Douglas rabbitbrush is a perennial with stems 10 to 24 inches tall. Its bark is brown. Leaves are narrow, usually twisted, green, smooth or short-hairy but never woolly or silky. A sticky secretion is usually found at the base of the leaves. Flowers are yellow, small, in rounded or flat-topped clusters.

Douglas rabbitbrush is a native shrub growing in similar habitats as gray rabbitbrush. It is often confused with broom snakeweed. However, Douglas rabbitbrush usually has twisted leaves whereas those of broom snakeweed are straight. In addition, broom snakeweed dies completely back to the ground each year, while Douglas rabbitbrush does not. Like gray rabbitbrush it is considered an undesirable increaser, which increases with overgrazing and is difficult to control.

Non-standard name: green rabbitbrush.

Leaves attach to brown-barked stems, having a spiral appearance. New growth comes from woody stems rather than the crown of the plant.

Flowers are yellow and appear as clusters in late summer and fall.

Chicory
Cichorium intybus L.

Chicory
Asteraceae
(Sunflower family)

Chicory is a perennial, with milky juice, growing from a deep taproot. Stems are 1 to 6 feet tall with spreading branches. Leaves are rough, basal leaves in rosette, oblanceolate, petiolate, toothed or often pinnately parted, and 2 to 10 inches long. Upper leaves become reduced, sessile, and even entire. Flowering heads are borne 1 to 3 together in the axils of much reduced upper leaves. Flowers are usually blue, but sometimes purple or occasionally white, up to 1 1/2 inches across. Fruits are weakly angled or ribbed, tipped by a crown of minute scales.

Chicory is a native of the Mediterranean region, but now it is cosmopolitan in the northern hemisphere. It is widespread along roadsides and disturbed sites, having been planted by man for use as salad greens and the root as a substitute for coffee. Flowering occurs from July to September.

Immature growth of chicory appears as a rosette with lobed leaves that are rough in appearance.

Flower heads up to 1 1/2 inches across are normally blue or purple, sometimes white, and appear in mid-summer. Flowers are square on the end and lobed.

Canada thistle
Cirsium arvense (L.) Scop.

Canada thistle
Asteraceae
(Sunflower family)

Canada thistle is a colony-forming perennial from deep and extensive horizontal roots. Stems are 1 to 4 feet tall, ridged, branching above. Leaves are alternate, lacking petioles, oblong or lance-shaped, divided into spiny-tipped irregular lobes. Flowers are unisexual, on separate plants; flowers purple (occasionally white) in heads 1/2 to 3/4 inch in diameter; involucral bracts spineless. Fruits are about 1/8 inch long, somewhat flattened, brownish, with a tuft of hairs at the top.

Canada thistle is a native of southeastern Eurasia. It was introduced to Canada as a contaminant of crop seed as early as the late 18th century. Canada thistle differs from other species of the true thistle in that there are male and female flower heads, and these are on separate plants. By asexual reproduction, it is possible that a colony of male plants would produce no fruits, but still maintain itself. This aggressive weed is difficult to control; for example, breaking up the roots by plowing only serves to increase the number of plants. Flowering occurs during July and August.

Early spring growth appears as rosettes with spiny-tipped, wavy leaves.

Clusters of purple flower heads up to 3/4 inch across appear in late summer on this perennial. Bracts under the flowers are spineless.

Platte thistle
Cirsium canescens Nutt.

Platte thistle
Asteraceae
(Sunflower family)

Platte thistle is a perennial reproducing from seed. Seedling plant leaves become lobed as they develop. The entire plant is covered with fine hair. Each leaf is deeply lobed with yellow spines at the tip of each lobe. Leaf margins have smaller spines. Flowers are cream-white with the bracts being covered by short yellow spines. Seeds are light colored and curved. Blooms appear in early summer with seed development completed by July.

Platte thistle is common along roadsides and in rangeland in the Rocky Mountain region but is not considered a threat to livestock forage production.

Early spring growth appears as a blue-green rosette with deeply lobed leaves.

White flowers appear on this perennial in mid-summer. Yellow spines are found on the rounded involucre under the flower.

Yellowspine thistle
Cirsium ochrocentrum Gray

Yellowspine thistle
Asteraceae
(Sunflower family)

This is a biennial or short-lived perennial, sometimes reproducing by tuberous offsets. Stems 2 1/2 to 4 1/2 feet tall, simple or sparingly branched above, and densely covered with short woolly hairs. Leaves are 3 to 8 inches long, greenish or grayish, with tufts of soft woolly hairs on the surface and densely pubescent with short woolly hairs on the underside. Leaves are pinnately cleft into narrow lobes not reaching to the midrib, with rather crowded segments, which are mostly directed towards apex and armed with long yellowish spines 1/8 to 1/4 inch long. Leaf margins are irregularly toothed and these spine-tipped. Flowers are purple, rose, or cream-colored, solitary and terminal. Involucral bracts are in 5 to 7 rows, with cobweb-like hairs at least on the margin, outer ones are egg-shaped to narrow with a dark glandular dorsal ridge and a spreading yellow spine-tip, and the inner ones lance-shaped. Achenes, tan to brownish, smooth, and have a white pappus attached.

Yellowspine thistle, native to the U.S., can be found in dry sandy and gravelly soil in prairies, pastures, and open disturbed sites in several of the western states.

Leaves are pubescent, pinnately cleft and armed with long yellowish spines.

Terminal, solitary flowers are purple, rose to cream-colored. Involucral bracts are somewhat covered with cobweb-like hairs and have a spreading yellow spine at the tip.

Leafy thistle
Cirsium foliosum (Hook.) DC.

Leafy thistle
Asteraceae
(Sunflower family)

An erect, taprooted, perennial growing 2 to 4 feet tall. Stems leafy, succulent, often with a few side branches. Stems and foliage are pale green, sometimes sparsely covered with thin cobwebby hairs. Leaves are deeply indented or toothed, with many narrow spine-tipped lobes. Flowers are white to light pink. Flowers are supported on short stalks in leaf axils, often appearing to attach directly to the main stem when blossoms first appear.

Leafy thistle is a native species, typically found in wet meadows, seeps, and pastures at mid to high elevations. At least 2 distinct varieties are reported. A unique feature is that the leaves surround the terminal flowers which are colored pink to white.

Non-standard names: elk thistle, Drummond's thistle, meadow thistle.

Flowers are light pink to white. Flower heads develop on short stalks in leaf axils; the leaves extending well beyond flowers.

Meadow thistle is typically found in wet pastures and meadows at mid to high elevations.

Wavyleaf thistle
Cirsium undulatum (Nutt.) Spreng.

Wavyleaf thistle
Asteraceae
(Sunflower family)

A perennial from a simple taproot. Stems are erect, branching, and 1 1/2 to 3 1/2 feet tall. Leaves of basal rosettes are 3 to 10 inches long, toothed, and hairy on both upper and lower surfaces, with spines 1/16 to 2 3/8 inches long. Upper leaves are also toothed and spined, but are smaller. Flowers may be pink, pink-purple, or creamy white. Flower bracts often have a prominent white glandular dorsal ridge, and are hairy on the margins or overall.

Wavyleaf thistle is a native species, often associated with sagebrush communities in foothills, meadows, and rangeland.

Non-standard name: gray thistle.

Wavyleaf thistle rosette.

Involucre bracts often have a prominent white glandular dorsal ridge and minutely hairy margins.

Bull thistle
Cirsium vulgare (Savi) Tenore

Bull thistle
Asteraceae
(Sunflower family)

Bull thistle is a biennial with a short, fleshy taproot. The stem is 2 to 5 feet tall, bearing many spreading branches. It is green or brownish, sparsely hairy, irregularly and spiny winged. Leaves in the first year form a rosette, stem leaves are pinnately lobed, hairy and prickly on upper side and cottony underneath. Flowers are 1 1/2 to 2 inches wide, more or less clustered at the ends of branches. Involucral bracts are narrow, spine-tipped, progressively longer and narrower from outer to inner ones, flowers dark purple. Seeds are topped by a circle of plume-like white hairs.

Bull thistle is a native of Eurasia and is now widely established in North America, having been introduced many times as a seed contaminant. Pastures, roadsides and disturbed sites are potential habitats for this highly competitive weed. Flowering occurs from July through September. It is possible to separate bull thistle from Canada thistle by examination of the leaves alone. Bull thistle leaves are prickly hairy above and cottony below, while Canada thistle leaves are glabrous above and glabrous or hairy below.

A rosette appears the first season of this biennial's life cycle. Leaves have prickles on the surface with margins deeply lobed and wavy.

Flowers are pinkish-purple and appear in mid-summer. The involucre is somewhat tapered and covered with spines.

119

Hairy fleabane
Conyza bonariensis (L.) Cronq.

Hairy fleabane
Asteraceae
(Sunflower family)

Annual 1/2 to 3 feet in height often confused with horseweed (*C. canadensis*). In early vegetative stages hairy fleabane has a more branching growth habit. Leaves are often slightly wrinkled or distorted, often hairy, 2 to 4 inches long and 1/4 to 1/2 inch wide with dark foliage. Heads are about 1/2 inch in diameter, and numerous, borne at the terminal ends of the stems and each composed of 50 to 100 disk and many ray flowers. The seed pappus at maturity is two times or more the length of the body of the seed.

Hairy fleabane is a native of the American tropics and is common throughout California in waste areas and cultivated fields. It is also known as flaxleaved fleabane.

Non-standard name: flaxleaved fleabane.

Flowers borne at the end of numerous branches.

Seedlings have narrow leaves which are typically hairy and often wrinkled.

121

Horseweed
Conyza canadensis (L.) Cronq.

Horseweed
Asteraceae
(Sunflower family)

Horseweed is a winter or summer annual, 1 to 5 feet tall. Stems are erect, unbranched below but often branched above. Leaves are alternate, crowded on the stem, simple, bristly with hairs and sessile or short petioled. Lower leaves are spatulate and sparingly or coarsely toothed, while upper leaves are lance-shaped to linear. The inflorescence is branched with slender flower stalks, flower heads are small with white ray and yellow disk flowers. Seeds are numerous, small, flattened, about 1/16 inch long, with a white bristly pappus.

A native of North American grasslands, horseweed is common in pastures, meadows, cultivated fields, along roadsides and in waste areas. Mowing infested meadows or pastures when the plants are in the bud stage will prevent seed production. The leaves and flowers contain a terpene which is particularly irritating in the nostrils of horses. Flowering and seed production occur from late June to September.

Stiff hairs cover the narrow leaves that are individually attached alternately around the stem.

Small, inconspicuous flowers are borne at stem terminals in mid-summer on this annual.

123

Bristly hawksbeard
Crepis setosa Haller f.

Bristly hawksbeard
Asteraceae
(Sunflower family)

Annual with a taproot. Stems which originate as one or several from the base are branched, 1 to 2+ feet tall and somewhat hairy. Stem leaves are broadest at the base and coarsely toothed or lobed. Heads are yellow, generally numerous and small. Bracts of the head are coarse and stiff bristled. Smooth hawksbeard (*C. capillaris* (L.) Wallr.) is similar in appearance but has smooth stems and leaves and lacks bristles.

Bristly hawksbeard was introduced from Europe and has become a common weed of lawns and waste areas.

Non-standard name: rough hawksbeard.

Small yellow flowers are often confused with those of spotted catsear (false dandelion) which has no leaves on the stems.

Bristly stems help to distinguish bristly hawksbeard from other species.

125

Common crupina
Crupina vulgaris Cass.

Common crupina
Asteraceae
(Sunflower family)

Common crupina is a fall germinating annual. The fleshy cotyledon has a red or purple midrib. Rosette leaves are obovate with entire to slightly toothed margins. Older rosette leaves and stem leaves are pinnately to bi-pinnately lobed. Margins of lobes are armed with short, stiff spines giving leaves a coarse, rough texture when touched. Stem leaves are alternate, sessile and progressively smaller toward the stem apex. Mature plant height varies from 1 to 3 feet. Main stem terminates in one to several short flowering branches; additional flowering branches originate in upper leaf axils. One to 5 flower heads produced on each branch. Heads are narrow, cylindric (3 to 4 times longer than wide) and topped with pink, lavender or purple flowers. A distinct ring of dark, stiff bristles encircle the broad end of the seed giving the appearance of a fishing dry fly.

Common crupina is native to the Mediterranean region. Found in range and disturbed non-crop lands in Idaho, Washington, California and Oregon. The primary Pacific Northwest habitat of common crupina is southern slopes in steep canyon grasslands. Flowering usually occurs from June to July.

Common crupina seedling showing the fleshy oblong cotyledons, the midrib often red or purple colored.

Mature flower heads terminate with purple ray flowers.

127

Lowland cudweed
Gnaphalium palustre Nutt.

Lowland cudweed
Asteraceae
(Sunflower family)

An annual plant grayish to white woolly with a spreading growth habit occasionally up to 12 inches tall. Leaves are alternate, entire and oblong, often broadly so, 3/8 to 3 3/8 inches long and 1/8 to 3/8 inches wide. Heads are small, about 1/8 inch high, and borne in leaf axils and at the ends of the branches.

This native plant is semi-weedy in moist open places after the area dries. Several similar species occur in the western United States.

Dense tufts of long woolly hair are characteristic of cudweed.

Brownish clusters of terminal heads.

Curlycup gumweed
Grindelia squarrosa (Pursh) Dunal

Curlycup gumweed
Asteraceae
(Sunflower family)

Curlycup gumweed is a biennial or short-lived perennial that reproduces by seed and grows 1 to 3 feet tall. The roots are fibrous; leaves alternate, 1 to 3 inches long, with saw-toothed margins. They are gland-dotted and exude a sticky material. Flower heads are bright yellow, 1 inch in diameter, borne singly on the end of the branches. Curved bracts surrounding the flower also secrete a sticky substance which gives the plant its name. Seeds are oblong, cream colored, four-angled and deeply ridged.

Curlycup gumweed is a native plant found in pastures, rangelands, roadsides and waste areas sometimes forming nearly pure stands. It is highly drought resistant and increases after periods of dryness. It is considered undesirable as forage and is unpalatable to livestock. Indians used gumweed as a treatment for asthma, bronchitis, colic and skin rash. Extracts of gumweed are used in today's medicine for treatment of bronchial spasm, asthma, whooping cough and poison ivy rashes.

Non-standard name: rosinweed.

Leaves are alternate and rounded with a toothed margin and are covered with a sticky resin.

Waxy yellow flowers appear in mid-summer on curlycup gumweed. The involucre surrounding the flower is covered with curved bracts which secrete a sticky resin.

131

Broom snakeweed
Gutierrezia sarothrae (Pursh) Britt. & Rusby

Broom snakeweed
Asteraceae
(Sunflower family)

Broom snakeweed is a native perennial warm-season plant reproducing by seed and root systems. The plant has a woody nature but rarely grows to heights over 18 inches. Stems grow new from the crown each year, not from old growth. Stems are close together, stiff and somewhat resinous. Leaves are alternate, narrow and untwisted, 1 to 1 1/2 inches long and are green with smooth margins, slightly rolled to the center and are located on the upper parts of the plant. Flower heads are small with inconspicuous yellow ray flowers. Fruit are oval and covered with chaffy scales. It is considered an evergreen shrub in New Mexico and Arizona but is deciduous in northern states.

Broom snakeweed is a common poisonous plant which is most toxic during leaf formation. Most losses occur in cattle and sheep as abortions. Weak calves and lambs are common during times when pasture is scarce and broom snakeweed is eaten. Pastures are not properly utilized when this weed is found intermixed with the grasses. Control of this species can be attained with herbicides.

Non-standard name: broomweed.

Spring growth of this perennial comes from the plant crown each year. Leaves are 1 to 1 1/2 inches long and are straight.

Small yellow flowers appear in mid-summer on this perennial.

133

Common sunflower
Helianthus annuus L.

Common sunflower and Nuttall sunflower
Asteraceae
(Sunflower family)

The common sunflower is an annual, 1 to 10 feet tall. Stems are erect, simple to much branched and rough. Leaves alternate and are simple, rough, hairy, ovate or heart-shaped, with toothed edges. The flowers are showy, with yellow to orange-yellow ray flowers and brown or dark reddish-brown disk flowers. Achenes, gray to brown, are 1/4 inch long, wedge-shaped, somewhat flattened to 4-angled, smooth except for a few short hairs at the tip.

Nuttall sunflower, *H. nuttallii* Torr. & Gray is a perennial, 2 to 10 feet tall. Smooth to rough stems grow erect, arising from a cluster of enlarged, tuberous roots with short, thick rhizomes. Leaves are opposite or sometimes nearly all alternate, ovate to narrowly lanceolate, with entire or serrated edges. The flower heads are few and at the end of long peduncles.

Native to North America, sunflowers have been cultivated since pre-Columbian times for its edible seeds. They are common weeds of roadsides, fence rows, fields, pastures, and waste areas. Flowering is from July to September.

Seedlings of common sunflower have a rough surface with a slightly lobed margin tapered to a point.

Clusters of flowers appear in late summer on Nuttall sunflower. Flower heads, approximately 2 inches across.

135

Texas blueweed
Helianthus ciliaris DC.

Texas blueweed
Asteraceae
(Sunflower family)

Texas blueweed is a perennial, 1 to 2 feet tall, with stems arising from woody, creeping roots. The sessile leaves are mostly opposite, narrow to broadly lance-shaped, 1 to 4 inches long, margins wavy, often with hairs. The flower head, 1/2 to 1 inch across, has involucral bracts egg- to oblong-shaped, either rounded or with short, sharp tips, and somewhat overlapping. Ray flowers are yellow, with disk flowers reddish to dark purple. Achenes are grayish brown, four-angled, somewhat wedge-shaped and about 1/8 inch long.

Texas blueweed is native to the southwestern U.S. and can be found in both cropland and disturbed areas.

Due to extensive underground creeping rootstalks Texas blueweed is an aggressive troublesome weed.

Opposite leaves, 1 to 4 inches long, are usually narrow, having wavy margins and often with hairs along the margins.

Spikeweed
Hemizonia pungens (Hook. & Arn.) T. & G.

Spikeweed
Asteraceae
(Sunflower family)

Spikeweed is an annual growing 1 1/2 to 3 feet tall, basal leaves pale straw colored, stiff, several inches long, with narrow lobes. Leaves along stem 1/2 inch long or less, sharp pointed, bearing dwarf vegetative branches or short flowering branches in their axils; heads borne at tips of short leafy branches, yellow, about 1/3 inch broad; fruit 1/16 inch long with wart-like projections and a short spine.

Spikeweed is native to California; it is abundant in the southern part of the state and has been reported in Washington and Oregon. It grows in dense clusters on alkaline soils on roadsides and waste areas, grain fields and in rangeland. Spikeweed is a tough, spiny plant which is avoided by livestock. It is a heavy seed producer and forms dense stands on areas favorable to its growth; flowering occurs from July to September.

Seedling plants have leaves which are several inches long and sharply divided.

Spikeweed flowers are surrounded with spiny bracts making plants undesirable for grazing.

139

Camphorweed
Heterotheca subaxillaris (Lam.) Britt. & Rusby

Camphorweed
Asteraceae
(Sunflower family)

Camphorweed is a tall, coarse, hairy, annual or biennial, with a strong, characteristic odor. The plant comes from a taproot and grows 2 to 6 feet tall. Stems are singular, mostly branching only at the top, more or less covered by long, spreading hairs with the upper branchlets and flower stalks bearing gland-tipped hairs. Leaves alternate with the lower leaves stalked, elliptic to lance-oblong, and usually with a pair of leaflike lobes on either side of the stalk base. The upper leaves are almost heart-shaped, sessile, and clasping the stem. Flower heads are relatively small, glandular, 1/2 to 3/4 inch in diameter. Ray flowers are yellow as are the disk flowers.

Camphorweed, native of tropical America, grows in moist or dry sandy soil in both crop and noncrop areas, and can be found in southwestern U.S. It is closely related to telegraphplant (*H. grandiflora* Nutt.), except the latter has larger flowers with pubescent ray achenes, and upper leaves usually narrowed at the base.

Upper leaves are sessile (as shown), while lower leaves are stalked.

Flowers are found in the upper portion of the plant and have both yellow ray and disk flowers.

141

Orange hawkweed
Hieracium aurantiacum L.

Orange hawkweed
Asteraceae
(Sunflower family)

Fibrous rooted perennial herb up to 12 inches tall. The leaves are basal, occasionally with 1 or 2 small leaves on the bristly stems. The plants contain milky juice. It has 5 to 30 flower heads, each in a compact umbelliform inflorescence. The strap-shaped flowers are red-orange with notched tips. Yellow hawkweed (*H. pratense* Tausch.) is similar in appearance to orange hawkweed.

The distribution of both species is limited. Orange hawkweed is reported to be west of the Cascades and into northwest Wyoming and yellow hawkweed in northeast Washington and adjacent Idaho.

Seedling showing bristly hairs.

Orange hawkweed's strap-shaped flowers have notched tips.

Spotted catsear
Hypochaeris radicata L.

Spotted catsear
Asteraceae
(Sunflower family)

Spotted catsear is a perennial, 3/4 to 2 feet tall. Leaves are 2 to 8 inches long, toothed or lobed, rough-hairy, borne in a basal rosette. Flowering stems are sparsely branching. Heads are 1 to 1 1/2 inches in diameter, the flowers yellow, all strap-shaped. Fruits are rough and long-beaked, tipped by a circle of plume-like bristles.

Spotted catsear is European in origin, and is now widely established in the U.S. and southern Canada. It is more prevalent west of the Cascade Mountains. It flowers from May to October. This is a weed of disturbed sites, waste areas, lawns, gardens, pastures and cultivated fields.

Non-standard name: false dandelion.

This perennial forms a rough-hairy rosette the first year.

Yellow strap-shaped flowers are found at the end of a 10 to 16 inch long stem.

145

Poverty sumpweed
Iva axillaris Pursh

Poverty sumpweed
Asteraceae
(Sunflower family)

Poverty sumpweed is a perennial, 6 to 18 inches tall. Stems are erect, much branched, smooth or slightly hairy. Leaves are mainly opposite, numerous, sessile, entire, narrowly oblong, 1/4 to 3/4 inch long, rough-hairy, harsh and stiff to the touch. The small tubular flowers are borne in small heads which hang from the axils of the upper leaves; achenes are deep gray to almost black, wedge-shaped, 1/8 inch long with a rough surface.

Native of western U.S., poverty sumpweed can be found from the Canadian border to Mexico. It commonly occurs along railroad rights-of-way and roadsides, in pastures and waste areas, and sometimes in cultivated cropland. It is quite tolerant of saline and alkaline soils.

Non-standard name: povertyweed.

Seedling plants have oval, rough opposite leaves.

Small, tubular yellow flowers borne in leaf axils are produced in late summer on this perennial.

147

Marshelder
Iva xanthifolia Nutt.

Marshelder
Asteraceae
(Sunflower family)

Marshelder is a robust branched annual, 2 to 10 feet tall and reproducing by seed. Leaves are mostly opposite; but the uppermost alternate, with long petioles. Blade is ovate to broadly ovate, 3 to 12 inches long and similar to those of common cocklebur. Flowering heads are similar to those of povertyweed; but they are stalkless, crowded on long, branching spikes at the top of the stem and the upper leaf axils. Flowers are greenish-white, with 8 to 20 staminate flowers and usually 5 pistillate flowers. Corollas are greatly reduced. Fruits are ovate, less than 1/4 inch long and dark brown.

Marshelder is an occasional weed in sandy, damp or drying sites, especially streambeds and flood plains. The pollen may cause serious hay fever in late summer, and the leaves produce a skin rash in some people. Flowering occurs from late July through September. It is native to middle North America.

Leaves, often over 6 inches across, have toothed margins with distinct veins on the surface. Opposite leaves are connected to the main stem with a long petiole.

Ovate fruit less than 1/4 inch long appear as a mealy substance surrounding the terminal stems.

149

Blue lettuce
Lactuca pulchella (Pursh) DC.

Blue lettuce
Asteraceae
(Sunflower family)

A deep-rooted rhizomatous perennial, with an erect leafy stem growing up to 4 feet tall. Leaves are 2 to 6 inches long, lance-shaped or linear, with lower leaves often prominently toothed. Leaves are smooth, bluish-green, with light midribs. Blue to purple flowers distinguish this from most other species of *Lactuca*. Seeds may be black or brown, with a short beak bearing a tuft of white hairs. Plants exude a white milky sap when injured.

Blue lettuce is a native of North America, but is considered a troublesome or noxious weed in some areas of the West. Typical habitat includes foothills, marshes, canals, streambanks, roadsides, meadows, pastures, and cultivated fields.

Blue to purple flowers, up to 1 inch in diameter, distinguish this from most other species of Lactuca.

Deep-growing vertical and lateral rootstocks.

Prickly lettuce
Lactuca serriola L.

Prickly lettuce
Asteraceae
(Sunflower family)

Prickly lettuce is a biennial or winter annual, from a taproot, with milky juice, reproducing only by seeds. Principal stem is 1 to 5 feet tall, branching only in flowering portion, or sometimes a few short branches from the base. Leaves alternate, twisted at the base to lie in a vertical plane, prickly on the lower side of the midrib, clasping the stem with two angled or earlike lobes. Lower leaves are 2 to 10 inches long with two forms. Margins may be pinnately lobed or lobeless. Flower heads are yellow, often drying blue, 1/8 to 1/3 inch broad and composed of ray flowers only. Each flowering head has 6 to 30 flattened fruits with 5 to 7 parallel ridges on each side. The fruit are bristly near the summit.

Prickly lettuce is a native of Europe, and is now naturalized throughout most of the U.S. This weed is a serious invader in disturbed soil of irrigated crops and orchards. It is also common along roadsides, yards and small gardens. Hybrids may represent an infusion of genes from cultivated lettuce. Flowering occurs from July to September.

Non-standard names: China lettuce, wild lettuce.

Leaves are slightly lobed in the seedling stage with sharp spines found on the back side of the midrib.

Small yellow flower heads less than 1/3 inch across are numerous on the terminal branches of this annual.

153

Nipplewort
Lapsana communis L.

Nipplewort
Asteraceae
(Sunflower family)

An annual with erect stems that are simple or branched above and are 4 inches to 4 feet in height. The leaves are broadly triangular to roundish, the lower leaves often with one to several small remote lobes. Leaves are long-stalked, upper leaves narrowing and borne on progressively shorter stalks. Leaf blades are irregularly toothed and soft hairy to smooth. Heads are several and borne at the tip of the branches; bracts are firm and erect; flowers are yellow.

Nipplewort is naturalized from Eurasia and is now a common weed in much of the U.S.

Broadly triangular leaf with irregularly toothed margin and soft to hairy blade.

Heads with upright bracts and yellow flowers.

Skeletonweed

Lygodesmia juncea (Pursh) D. Don

Skeletonweed
Asteraceae
(Sunflower family)

Skeletonweed is a perennial reproducing by seed. The plant grows up to 18 inches tall and appears to be all stems. The stems are erect, green, finely grooved and branched. Leaves are small, linear and up to two inches long at the base. Upper leaves are reduced to small awl-like projections. Stems and leaves contain a white, milky, latex sap. Light purple flower heads are less than one inch across and flattened, but lobed at the tip. Seeds are less than 1/2 inch long, have eight to 10 ridges vertically and have a cream-colored pappus. Blooms appear in late June through September with seeds maturing in July to September.

Skeletonweed is common along roadsides, waste areas, pastures, rangeland and in cropland. It is not controlled by most herbicides; therefore, it appears to be increasing in density in many areas. This plant could become a potential problem in cropland, so prevention would be advisable.

Upper leaves on skeletonweed are reduced to small awl-like projections.

Skeletonweed produces light purple flowers in late summer. Flowers have teeth on the tips.

157

Purple aster
Machaeranthera canescens (Pursh) Gray

Purple aster
Asteraceae
(Sunflower family)

Purple aster, white prairieaster (*Aster falcatus* Lindl.) and hairy goldenaster (*Heterotheca villosa* Pursh.) are usually perennials, 1/2 to 2 feet in height, reproducing by seed and white prairieaster by underground creeping roots. Leaves vary from sparsely to densely hairy, fleshy and firm with linear-lanceolate shape, 1 to 2 inches long. Flowers are clustered at ends of branches with over 20 white, yellow or purple flowers per inflorescence. Flowering occurs from July to October.

Many aster species occur in the West. Most are not considered problem species but under damp soil moisture conditions can be very competitive in meadows, rangeland or home landscapes.

White prairieaster is less common than purple aster but often grows near the same location.

Hairy goldenaster flowers are often larger than purple or white prairieaster. Leaves and stems are extremely hairy.

Coast tarweed
Madia sativa Molina

Coast tarweed
Asteraceae
(Sunflower family)

An annual with erect stems, up to 5 feet tall. Stems are leafy, simple or branching and the entire plant is sticky – glandular, disagreeably scented and hairy. Leaves are narrow. Flowering heads are inconspicuous and clustered at the apex of the stem, at ends of branches and in leaf axils. Heads are always partially enclosed by leaves. Ray flowers are few, short and yellow.

Coast tarweed was introduced from South America and can now be found from Washington to California. It occurs along roadsides, in disturbed areas, and on dry open hillsides, and overgrazed rangeland.

Non-standard name: Chilean tarweed.

Resinous material on flower and leaves of coast tarweed.

Resinous leaves, stem, and head of coast tarweed.

Pineapple-weed
Matricaria matricarioides (Less.) C.L. Porter

Pineapple-weed
Asteraceae
(Sunflower family)

Annual which is decumbent, up to 1+ feet tall with leaves that are greatly divided into very short narrow segments. The heads are cone-shaped, 1/16 to 1/3 inch high with many yellowish-green flowers, each head surrounded by several overlapping bracts with papery margins. The ray flowers are lacking. Pineapple-weed gives off a pleasant "pineapple" odor when plants are crushed.

Pineapple-weed is native to North America and is a common pest of roadsides, gardens, and cropland. Mayweed chamomile (*Anthemis cotula* L.) has a similar appearance but has a disagreeable odor and white ray flowers.

Note the absence of ray flowers on the heads of pineapple-weed.

A typical patch of pineapple-weed.

163

Scotch thistle
Onopordum acanthium L.

Scotch thistle
Asteraceae
(Sunflower family)

Scotch thistle is a biennial that grows up to 12 feet tall. Stems have broad, spiny wings. Leaves are large, spiny, and covered with fine dense hair, giving a grayish appearance. Upper leaves are alternate, coarsely lobed; basal leaves may be up to 2 feet long and 1 foot wide. Flower heads are numerous, 1 to 2 inches in diameter, bracts spine-tipped. Flowers are violet to reddish. Fruits are about 3/16 inch long, tipped with slender bristles.

Scotch thistle is a native of Europe and eastern Asia and is now sparsely naturalized over much of the U.S. It can be found along waste areas and roadsides. It is an aggressive plant and may form stands so dense that they are impenetrable to livestock. Scotch thistle is best controlled in the rosette stage.

Non-standard name: cotton thistle.

Rosettes two feet across are not uncommon for this hearty plant. Leaves are covered with white hair giving them a blue-green color.

Violet to reddish flowers, 1 to 2 inches in diameter, are produced the second year of this biennial's growth cycle. Stems appear to have wings.

165

Tansy ragwort
Senecio jacobaea L.

Tansy ragwort
Asteraceae
(Sunflower family)

Tansy ragwort is a biennial or short-lived perennial from a taproot. Stems are 1 to 6 feet tall, solitary or several, simple up to the inflorescence. Their pubescence consists of cobwebby hairs in early stages of growth. Leaves 2 to 8 inches long, alternate and equally distributed, mostly 2 to 3 times pinnately lobed, the terminal lobe generally larger than the lateral ones. Flowering heads are numerous. Both ray and disk flowers are yellow; ray flowers are 10 to 13 in number and 1/4 to 1/2 inch long. Fruits of the disk flowers are minutely pubescent; those of the ray flowers are glabrous.

This European native is widespread in Washington, Oregon and California, having arrived in seaports in the early 1900s. Tansy ragwort is toxic to cattle and horses. Like common groundsel, it has several alkaloids which produce irreversible liver damage. Flowering occurs from July to September. While tansy ragwort is not presently in all the western states, it does infest millions of acres of private range, public range and pasture land in the Pacific Northwest.

Rosettes of this biennial have leaves that are deeply lobed – compound leaflets are also lobed.

Yellow terminal flower heads less than 1 inch across are borne as terminal clusters on tansy ragwort.

167

Riddell groundsel
Senecio riddellii Torr. & Gray

Riddell groundsel
Asteraceae
(Sunflower family)

A perennial subshrub 12 to 40 inches tall. Stems are numerous, arching and branching upward from a taprooted woody crown. Divided leaves less than 3/16 inch in width are often over 3 inches long and without hairs. Thread-leaf groundsel (*S. longilobus* Benth.) has a similar appearance but has a gray color caused by fine hairs covering the leaf. Broom groundsel (*S. spartioides* Torr. & Gray) (pictured) looks similar but leaves are undivided. Stems of threadleaf groundsel branch above the crown. Flowers appear from August to October.

Riddell groundsel and threadleaf groundsel are poisonous to cattle and sheep with poisoning being caused by pyrrolizidine alkaloids preventing reproduction of liver cells. Riddell groundsel is common on sandy moist sites while threadleaf groundsel typically grows in dry well-drained soils.

Riddell groundsel has divided leaves with flowers the same color and size as broom groundsel.

Broom groundsel has undivided leaves but are similar in size and shape to Riddell groundsel.

Common groundsel
Senecio vulgaris L.

Common groundsel
Asteraceae
(Sunflower family)

Common groundsel is a simple or branched annual, sometimes biennial, from a taproot. Stems are 6 to 18 inches tall; herbage is glabrous to crisp-hairy. Leaves are alternate, coarsely and irregularly toothed or pinnately parted. Basal leaves are usually purplish on the under-surface, 1 to 4 inches long and 1/2 to 1 1/2 inches wide. Heads are several to numerous, with yellow disk flowers; involucral bracts are black-tipped. Fruits are slender, ridged, somewhat pubescent, long, silky. White hairs terminate the achene. The genus *Senecio* is one of the largest genera of plants, containing well over 1000 species.

Woodland groundsel (*Senecio sylvaticus* L.) is also an annual which has similar flowers to common groundsel but has a nauseating odor when bruised and grows up to 3 1/2 feet tall with upper stems branched.

Seedlings appear as tiny rosettes with sharply notched leaves.

Woodland groundsel has small ray flowers and upper stems are branched.

Blessed milkthistle
Silybum marianum (L.) Gaertn.

Blessed milkthistle
Asteraceae
(Sunflower family)

Biennial or winter annual with stout, ridged, and generally branching stems up to 6 feet tall. Leaves sometimes reach 1+ feet in length and are broad, lobed and clasping the stem with ear-like lobes at the base. Leaves have spiny margins with white marbling along the veins. The head is thistle-like, with leathery spine-tipped bracts. The flowers are red purple.

This spectacular native of Europe is distributed widely in the West.

Long spines and large flower head of blessed milkthistle.

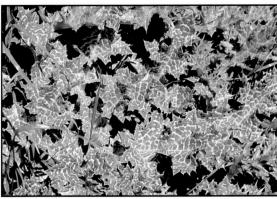

Spiny margins and white marbling along the veins of the leaves.

173

Canada goldenrod
Solidago canadensis L.

Canada goldenrod
Asteraceae
(Sunflower family)

Canada goldenrod is a perennial growing to heights of 4 feet, spreading by creeping roots and seeds. Alternate leaves surround the central stems and are gradually reduced upwards. Leaf blades are entire or commonly toothed and have three veins on the upper surface. Flowers are yellow, borne on numerous small heads with overlapping involucral bracts. Thirteen ray flowers are common, but there may be as few as 10 or as many as 17. Seeds are tipped with a circle of white hairs. *Solidago* is a genus of nearly 100 species, several common in the western U.S.

Canada goldenrod, a native of North America, is common in the U.S. and Canada. The plant is often seen along roadsides, streambanks and along ditches. The extensive root system makes it a difficult plant to control. It seldom reaches densities that are a problem in rangeland. Flowering occurs from August to October.

Leaves are alternately spaced, 3 to 5 inches in length. They have three distinct veins and are sometimes toothed.

Golden yellow flowers grow in clusters on the terminal stem in late summer.

Perennial sowthistle

Sonchus arvensis L.

Perennial sowthistle
Asteraceae
(Sunflower family)

A perennial, spreading from horizontal rhizome-like roots. Plants are usually 2 to 4 feet tall, succulent, and exude a milky juice when injured. Leaves have a clasping base and mildly prickly margins which vary from deeply toothed to nearly entire. Upper leaves are fewer and much smaller than the basal ones. The flower head is 1 to 2 inches wide, and rich yellow in color. Numerous gland-tipped hairs on involucre bracts and flower stalks help distinguish this species. Seeds are dark brown, prominently ridged and wrinkled, with a tuft of soft white pappus bristles.

Perennial sowthistle is a native of Europe or Eurasia. It is widely distributed in North America, and considered noxious in many states and provinces. It is common in gardens, cultivated crops, ditchbanks, and fertile waste areas where adequate water is available. Marsh sowthistle (listed by various authors as *S. uliginosus* Bieb., *S. arvensis* L. ssp. *uliginosus* (Bieb.) Nyman, or *S. glabrescens* Jord.) is a similar perennial; the most important difference being a lack of gland-tipped hairs.

Rich yellow flower heads may be up to 2 inches wide. Flower stalks and bracts are covered with gland-tipped hairs.

New shoots emerge from stout lateral roots.

Marsh sowthistle

Sonchus arvensis L. ssp. *uliginosus* (Bieb.) Nyman

Marsh sowthistle
Asteraceae
(Sunflower family)

This perennial arising from an extensive creeping root system is commonly 1 to 6 feet tall, glabrous, at least below the inflorescence and often covered with a waxy bloom which can be rubbed off. Herbage has a milky juice. Leaves are prickly-margined, the lower and middle ones are usually pinnately lobed to pinnatifid, mostly 4 to 10 inches long and 1 to 1 1/2 inches wide. Upper leaves are progressively less lobed and become clasping, uppermost leaves bractlike. Flowering heads, 1 to 1 1/2 inches across at anthesis, grow in a terminal flat to a domelike cluster. It has yellow ray flowers, which are fertile. Achenes are flattened, ribbed and rugose, with pappus of capillary bristles.

Marsh sowthistle was introduced from Europe and is a creeping perennial. Marsh sowthistle (listed by various authors as *S. uliginosus* or *S. glabrescens*) lacks gland-tipped hairs.

Leaves have sharp prickles on their lobed margins. Immature growth stages often come from extensive underground roots.

Yellow flowers appear in late summer which develop into a cluster of windblown seeds.

Spiny sowthistle
Sonchus asper (L.) Hill

Spiny sowthistle
Asteraceae
(Sunflower family)

A stout annual with stems 1 to 5 feet in height. The plant contains a milky juice. Lower leaves are lobed and toothed, the margins very spiny; leaves of the stem have sharp, stiff prickles and large rounded basal lobes clasping the stem. Flowers are yellow, all strap-shaped and are 3/4 to 1 inch in diameter. Fruits are reddish-brown, flattened and with 3 to 5 ribs on each face, with a cluster of fine white hairs attached to the upper end.

Spiny sowthistle, a native of Europe, has spread to become common in distribution. The flowering period is from July to October. The plant is found along roadsides and in waste areas, gardens, and cultivated fields.

Spiny sowthistle forms a rosette following germination, with leaves lobed and margins very spiny.

Yellow strap-shaped flowers are followed by a vase-like structure with ribbed fruit.

Annual sowthistle

Sonchus oleraceus L.

Annual sowthistle
Asteraceae
(Sunflower family)

An erect fleshy annual 1 to 4 feet high. Basal leaves are stalked while upper leaves clasp the stems. All but the upper leaves are deeply lobed with 1 to 3 lobes along each side. Flower heads are numerous and pale yellow, 1/4 to 3/4 inch wide. The seeds are flat and ribbed lengthwise with a tuft of fine hairs which allows wind-borne dissemination.

Sowthistle was introduced from Europe and is found throughout the western United States growing in vacant lots, roadsides, cultivated fields and gardens.

Non-standard name: sowthistle.

Flower head of annual sowthistle illustrating its involucre and numerous yellow flowers.

Mature seed head containing seeds with parachute-like pappus attached, facilitating windblown dissemination.

Common tansy
Tanacetum vulgare L.

Common tansy
Asteraceae
(Sunflower family)

Common tansy is an aromatic perennial. Stems are 1 1/2 to 6 feet tall. It reproduces from seeds and rootstalks. Leaves are alternate, deeply divided into numerous narrow, toothed segments. Yellow flower heads, 1/4 to 1/2 inch across, are numerous in flat-topped dense clusters. Seeds are yellowish-brown with short 5-toothed crowns.

Common tansy is a native of Europe and became established in the U.S. when introduced as an ornamental and for medicinal purposes. It is generally found along roadsides, waste areas, streambanks, and in pastures throughout most of the U.S. It is undesirable as forage for livestock. However, it has long been used as a medicinal herb. Common tansy is sometimes mistaken for tansy ragwort.

Non-standard name: garden tansy.

Leaves are divided into individual leaflets, which are serrated on the margins. Stems are often purplish-red in color.

Flower heads contain button-like flowers without petals.

Dandelion
Taraxacum officinale Weber in Wiggers

Dandelion
Asteraceae
(Sunflower family)

Dandelion is a perennial herb with milky juice from an often branched tap-root up to several feet long. Reproduces by seeds and by new shoots from the root crowns. Leaves are clustered at the top of the root crown. They vary in size, from 2 to 12 inches long, divided into pairs of lobes, which are pointed or blunt at the tips. The flower heads are 1 to 2 inches across, composed of yellow petal-like ray flowers. Heads are solitary. Achenes are 1/8 inch long, five- to eight-ribbed, the apex ends in a slender beak two or four times as long as the body of the achene, with parachute-like hairs at its apex. The genus *Taraxacum* is a taxonomically confusing group subject to many interpretations as to the number of species. In fact, hundreds of specific names have been published.

The common dandelion is native to Europe, but is now cosmopolitan. It grows in moist sites, including lawns, meadows, pastures and overgrazed areas. It is good forage on the ranges, and is especially relished by sheep and cattle. Flowering occurs almost nine months of the year.

Seedlings and immature growth stages of this perennial have leaves that vary in size from 2 to 12 inches long and are usually deeply lobed.

Yellow flowers on this perennial develop into a showy, circular ball of windblown seeds.

187

Spineless horsebrush
Tetradymia canescens DC.

Spineless horsebrush
Asteraceae
(Sunflower family)

Spineless horsebrush is a perennial, deciduous shrub growing from 1/2 to 3 feet tall. Leaves are simple, alternate, linear and woolly with a prominent midrib. Flowers are borne in terminal clusters and are yellow to cream-colored. Flower heads usually have 4 involucral bracts. Stems are short, stout and silvery canescent until maturity then become glabrous; nodes are prominent causing a "knobby" appearance.

Spineless horsebrush is a native rangeland plant and is common throughout rangelands of the West. It causes photosensitization in sheep, an allergic reaction of the skin caused by exposure to sunlight, symptoms of which are called "big head" from swelling of the head and facial features. Horsebrush causes severe liver damage when large amounts are eaten, and sheep may die within a day or two, while small amounts cause various degrees of photosensitivity to develop. Control measures for horsebrush have not been successful.

Non-standard name: gray horsebrush.

Spineless horsebrush plants are often confused with various sagebrush species before flowering. Leaves are linear and covered with dense hairs.

Flowering occurs in August and September with flowers ranging from yellow to cream-colored.

Western salsify
Tragopogon dubius Scop.

Western salsify
Asteraceae
(Sunflower family)

A biennial, 1 to 3 feet tall, more or less branched, arising from a long taproot. Herbage has milky juice. Some pubescence occurs when young, but is frequently glabrous at maturity. Leaves are narrow, up to 12 inches long, gradually tapering from the base to the apex. Flower heads occur at the end of long, hollow peduncles; involucral bracts, usually about 13, or only eight in depauperate plants, 1 to 2 inches long at anthesis. Bracts distinctly surpass the pale, lemon-yellow ray flowers. Achenes have a 1 inch or larger slender beak at the apex.

Western salsify is native to Eurasia and is now established over much of temperate North America. This is a weed of roadsides and waste sites. Other species of this genus are also common in the West, and sometimes species hybridize with each other. The stalk of meadow salsify (*T. pratensis* L.) is not swollen below the flower, while common salsify (*T. porrifolius* L.) has purple flowers.

Non-standard name: yellow salsify and goatsbeard.

Seedling and immature stages of salsify have long, narrow leaves containing a white milky juice.

The stalk of western salsify is swollen below the flower head.

Spiny cocklebur
Xanthium spinosum L.

Spiny cocklebur
Asteraceae
(Sunflower family)

An annual with spreading or erect stems, up to 2 feet long. Leaves are densely covered below with short white hairs and white-veined above, blades 1 to 3 inches long, narrow, generally with 2 short basal lobes or teeth, and a stiff 3-forked spine at the junction with the stem. Male flowers are uppermost and clustered. Female flowers are below the male flowers and form the bur. The fruit or "bur" bears a beak with hooked bristles.

Spiny cocklebur was introduced from Europe and is not as widely distributed as broadleaved cocklebur. Habitats include dry areas and barnyards.

Stem with 3-forked spines and burs.

Male flowers in clusters at top of plant.

Common cocklebur
Xanthium strumarium L.

Common cocklebur
Asteraceae
(Sunflower family)

Common cocklebur, an annual, 2 to 4 feet tall with the stem erect, branched, ridged, spotted and very rough. Leaves alternate, triangular or heart-shaped, rough on both sides and long petioled. Flower heads are small, in axils of upper leaves; male and female flowers are separate. Fruits are 1 inch long, woody, with hooked prickles and two curved spines at the tip and two seeds. Dark brown seeds are flattened and pointed on tips.

Common cocklebur is native to North America, but is now worldwide in distribution. Several other species are present in the West. Cocklebur is common in cultivated fields, abandoned land, run-down pastures, road ditches and waste areas. The burs are irritating both to humans and animals, and when found in wool, depreciate its value. Both the seeds and seedlings contain a substance toxic to livestock. Flowering may occur from July to September.

Seedling plants have very rough leaves that are notched on the margins and taper to a point. Careful removal of seedlings reveals the old bur from which it came which can be used for positive identification.

Large rough leaves are attached to a thick purplish-green stem with distinctive purple to black spots.

195

Woodyaster
Xylorhiza glabriuscula Nutt.

Woodyaster
Asteraceae
(Sunflower family)

Woodyaster is a perennial with numerous unbranched stems less than 12 inches tall, arising from a single crown and extensive, woody roots. Leaves are entire, lance-shaped, with finely toothed margins, tipped with fine spines. Flower heads are at the top of each stem, ray flowers petal-like, white to off-white with yellow disk flowers. The numerous seeds are topped by a tuft of brown hairs.

Woodyaster is a native rangeland species in the Rocky Mountain region and is an indicator of selenium soils. Livestock can be poisoned by this plant if consumed over extended periods. Decomposition of the woodyaster plants leaves selenium in a form readily absorbed by surrounding desirable vegetation.

Roots of this perennial are very large and woody. Plants grow to heights under 12 inches.

Flowers appear in early summer resembling small daisies with white ray flowers and yellow disk flowers in their center.

197

Coast fiddleneck
Amsinckia intermedia Fisch. & Mey

Coast fiddleneck
Boraginaceae
(Borage family)

An erect annual with bristly or hairy stems 1 to 2 1/2 feet in height. Leaves are alternate, ovate or strap-shaped and bristly hairy, 1 to 4 inches long. Flowers are yellow and grouped along one side of a terminal inflorescence which curls at the tip having a fiddleneck appearance. The calyx and corolla are 5-lobed, corolla funnel-shaped with 5 stamens attached to the tube. Fruit is 4-lobed and breaks apart at maturity, forming 4 nutlets, each one-seeded.

Coast fiddleneck is a native of California and Oregon and is found in cultivated fields flowering in late spring. A related species is tarweed fiddleneck (*A. lycopsoides* Lehm.) which can be distinguished by well developed fornices (internal appendages in the upper throat of the corolla). Hay containing fiddleneck has been shown to be poisonous to livestock.

Non-standard name: fiddleneck.

The yellow flowers are arranged on one side of a coiled axis.

Each lobe of the fruit contains a single seeded nutlet.

199

Catchweed
Asperugo procumbens L.

Catchweed
Boraginaceae
(Borage family)

A weak-stemmed, somewhat viny, annual with rough-textured leaves and stems which are covered with small, stiff bristly hairs that readily cling to animals and clothing. Flowers are small, blue to deep violet. The coarsely-toothed green calyx becomes much enlarged after flowering, forming a veiny, flattened sheath surrounding a cluster of 4 small nutlets.

Catchweed is an introduced species from Europe that is rapidly becoming a common weed of roadsides, waste places and cultivated areas.

Purple flowers are inconspicuous and short-lived.

Enlarged coarsely-toothed calyx and stiff recurved stem bristles.

Houndstongue
Cynoglossum officinale L.

Houndstongue
Boraginaceae
(Borage family)

Houndstongue is a biennial growing 1 to 4 feet tall and reproducing by seed. Leaves are alternate, 1 to 12 inches long, 1 to 3 inches wide, rough, hairy, and lacking teeth or lobes. Flowers are reddish-purple and terminal. The fruit is composed of 4 prickly nutlets each about 1/3 inch long.

Houndstongue was introduced from Europe. It forms a rosette the first year and sends up a flowering stalk the second year. The leaves are rough and resemble a hound's tongue. It may be found in pastures, along roadsides and in disturbed habitats. The nutlets break apart at maturity and cling to clothing or animals. Houndstongue is toxic, containing pyrrolizidine alkaloids, causing liver cells to stop reproducing. Animals may survive for six months or longer after they have consumed a lethal amount. Sheep are more resistant to houndstongue poisoning than are cattle or horses. Horses may be especially affected when confined in a small area infested with houndstongue and lacking desirable forage. Therefore, ranges and pastures should be maintained to encourage production of grasses and high quality forage.

Rosettes form in the first year of the two year growth cycle. Herbicides are most effective when applied at this growth stage.

In the second year, houndstongue plants flower and produce an abundant supply of seeds that spread by attaching to clothing or animals.

Western sticktight
Lappula occidentalis (S. Wats.) Greene

Western sticktight
Boraginaceae
(Borage family)

This annual, reproducing by seed, grows 6 to 12 inches tall. Leaves are narrow, somewhat blunt-tipped. Flowers are numerous, very small, blue to nearly white. Fruit is divided into 4 nutlets, margins covered with a single row of spear-like spines.

Western sticktight is native to the western plains region and is common along roadsides, waste areas, and abused ranges. The spiny seed, becoming entangled in wool, makes it a problem for sheep ranchers. It also readily clings to any passerby, so it is easily distributed.

Synonym: *Lappula redowskii* Am. auctt., Non (Hornem.) Greene.

Seedlings from this annual plant have oblong leaves covered with hair.

Western sticktight produces an abundant supply of seed from midsummer to fall. Seed is about 1/8 inch in size, spread by clinging to animals and clothing.

Corn gromwell
Lithospermum arvense L.

Corn gromwell
Boraginaceae
(Borage family)

Annual with erect stems that are slender and simple or branching at the base, 1/4 to over 2 feet tall. Leaves are lanceolate and usually without stalks. Flowers are white to bluish-white, borne in the axils of reduced upper leaves. The fruit is composed of 4 small erect nutlets, gray-brown, pitted and sometimes warty.

Introduced from Europe and now common throughout the U.S. Corn gromwell is especially troublesome where winter grains are grown.

Seedlings have lance-shaped leaves, a good identification characteristic of corn gromwell.

Flowers are borne in the axils of upper bracts.

Yellow alyssum
Alyssum alyssoides L.

Yellow alyssum
Brassicaceae
(Mustard family)

A spreading to erect annual growing 3 to 10 inches tall. Plants normally branch at the base. Leaves are narrow and strap-like, 1/4 to 1 inch long, lacking petioles. Leaves and stems are usually covered with tiny star-shaped hairs. Flowers are small, yellow fading to white, in many-flowered racemes at the tops of stems. Fruits are small, round, flattened silicles with thin wings on the margins and a slight notch at the apex.

Yellow alyssum was introduced from Europe. It is common in dry gravelly waste areas, foothills, and cropland. Dwarf alyssum (*A. desertorum* Stapf) and field alyssum (*A. minus* (L.) Rothm.) are other introduced weedy species that resemble yellow alyssum.

Early seedling stage showing cotyledons and first pairs of true leaves.

Advanced seedling stage showing leaf arrangement and decumbent nature.

Wintercress
Barbarea orthoceras Ledeb.

Wintercress
Brassicaceae
(Mustard family)

A biennial, perennial or sometimes winter annual that is dark green, erect, simple or branching and up to 2 feet tall. The lower leaves are generally rounded with a few small lobes and are usually shed by flowering time. Other leaves are generally divided into numerous lobes or leaflets, the terminal leaflet or lobe rounded or somewhat elongated and usually much larger than the small lateral structures. Flowers are at first borne in clusters at the tips of the stems, but elongate as the plant matures. The yellow petals are under 3/16 inch in length. Fruits are slender, 3/4 to 2 1/4 inches long.

Yellow flowers clustered at the stem terminal.

Leaves divided into numerous lobes or leaflets having a large, rounded terminal lobe.

Wild mustard
Brassica kaber (DC.) L.C. Wheeler

Wild mustard
Brassicaceae
(Mustard family)

An annual or winter annual 1 to 3 feet tall. Stems are erect, with stiff hairs, at least on lower portions. Leaves are 2 to 8 inches long, 1 to 4 inches wide, lower ones deeply lobed, upper leaves are merely toothed and may be short-stalked or stalkless (but not clasping). Flowers are yellow with 4 petals. Seed pods (siliques) lack hairs, are 1 1/4 to 2 inches long, oval to round in cross section, and supported on short (1/10 to 3/10 inch) pedicels. Seedpods have a constricted beak above the uppermost seed. The beak of wild mustard is 3/10 to 6/10 inch long, obviously flattened (2-edged or 4-angled), and valves (pod halves) each have 3 to 5 prominent lengthwise veins. Pods are somewhat spreading. White mustard (*B. hirta* Moench) resembles wild mustard, except that pods and pedicels of white mustard are covered with coarse spreading hairs.

Wild mustard, also called charlock mustard or kaber mustard, has been classified as *B. arvensis* (L.) Rabenh., *Sinapis arvensis* L., and *S. kaber* DC. by various authors. It is adventive from Europe; now widespread, infesting roadsides, cultivated fields, ditchbanks, and waste areas.

Flower cluster and leaf. Leaf shapes are not a reliable characteristic for distinguishing between Brassica *species.*

The seedpods of wild mustard have an angular constricted beak above the uppermost seed.

Black mustard
Brassica nigra (L.) Koch

Black mustard
Brassicaceae
(Mustard family)

An annual growing 2 to 8 feet tall. Stems are erect, with a sparse to dense covering of stiff hairs on lower portions, but generally smooth on upper stems. Leaves are 2 to 10 inches long, 1 to 6 inches wide, usually with a few short, stiff, scattered hairs. Leaves are stalked (not clasping, as in *B. rapa* L.), the lower ones deeply lobed and upper leaves toothed. Seed pods (siliques) lack hairs, are 4/10 to 1 inch long, somewhat 4-sided in cross-section, and supported on short (1/8 to 1/4 inch) pedicels. As with other *Brassica* species, pods have a conspicuous constricted beak above the uppermost seed. The beak of black mustard is short (1/20 to 1/4 inch) and cylindrical. Pod halves each have a single prominent lengthwise vein. Mature pods remain appressed close to the stem. Indian mustard (*B. juncea* (L.) Czern. & Coss.) resembles black mustard but has smooth leaves, longer pods, a longer beak (1/4 to 1/2 inch), and longer pedicels (3/10 to 7/10 inch), with ascending non-appressed pods.

This European introduction is widespread in North America, infesting roadsides, cultivated fields, other disturbed sites.

Non-standard name: short-pod mustard.

Flowers resemble those of other Brassica *species, having 4 bright yellow petals.*

Black mustard seed pods (top) are appressed close to the stem. Seed pods of B. kaber *(DC.) Wheeler (bottom) are larger and spreading.*

Birdsrape mustard
Brassica rapa L.

Birdsrape mustard
Brassicaceae
(Mustard family)

A winter annual or biennial growing 1 to 4 feet tall. Roots resemble a small turnip. Stems and foliage are usually smooth. Lower leaves are up to a foot long, with a large terminal lobe and smaller lateral lobes. Upper leaves are small and non-lobed, having a pointed tip and broad clasping base. Flowers are yellow with 4 petals. Seed pods (siliques) lack hairs, are 1 1/5 to 2 4/5 inches long, and supported on long (3/10 to 8/10 inch) pedicels. Seeds are black and nearly round. As with other *Brassica* species, pods have a conspicuous constricted beak above the uppermost seed. The beak of birdsrape mustard is 3/10 to 6/10 inch long, and valves (pod halves) each have a single (rather than 3 to 5) prominent lengthwise vein. Pods are spreading, rather than tightly appressed against the stem.

Birdsrape mustard was previously classified as *B. campestris* L. It is a native of Europe; now widespread in North America, infesting cultivated fields, roadsides, and waste areas.

Non-standard names: birds rape, wild mustard, wild turnip, wild rutabaga.

Showy 4-petalled yellow flower, typical of Brassica *mustards.*

Clasping upper leaves distinguish birdsrape mustard from other common mustards.

Smallseed falseflax
Camelina microcarpa Andrz. ex DC.

Smallseed falseflax
Brassicaceae
(Mustard family)

This is an annual, 1 to 3 feet in height. Leaves are alternate, simple, entire, clasping at the base of the stem. Pubescence is either forked or stellate. Flowers are in racemes; petals are pale yellow with fruit pod having several reddish-brown seeds in each chamber.

Smallseed falseflax was introduced from Europe. It is found on disturbed sites such as fields, roadsides and waste places. It is frequently brought into a new area with feeds. Smallseed falseflax produces seeds from late spring to early summer.

An immature plant shows the alternate leaf arrangement and entire leaves.

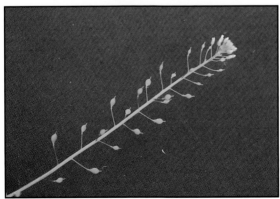

Reddish-brown seeds are contained in each of the oval capsules. Flower petals are pale yellow.

Shepherdspurse
Capsella bursa-pastoris (L.) Medic.

Shepherdspurse
Brassicaceae
(Mustard family)

Winter annual or annual, 3 to 18 inches tall with stems erect, slender, one to several from a basal rosette, hairy below and smooth above. Leaves are alternate with the lower ones usually deeply lobed, the upper ones are few, lance-shaped, toothed or entire, clasping the stem with a pair of ear-like lobes at the base. The flowers are white, small and usually found at the end of elongated racemes. Fruits more or less heart-shaped, two-celled; seeds many, very small, oblong, reddish-brown with a single ridge on each side.

Native of Europe, shepherdspurse has become well-established throughout much of the U.S. and Canada. It is common in cultivated fields, gardens, waste areas, poorly maintained pastures and on roadsides. This plant is one of the first to flower in the spring. Flowering and seed production may occur from April to September.

Seedlings of this winter annual are deeply lobed, forming a rosette.

Fruits are heart-shaped and contain many reddish-brown seeds. Heart-shaped capsules have a ridge down each face and are attached by a long pedicel to the main stem.

221

Hoary cress
Cardaria draba (L.) Desv.

Hoary cress
Brassicaceae
(Mustard family)

A deep rooted perennial up to 2 feet tall, reproducing from root segments and seeds. Leaves are blue-green in color, lance-shaped. Lower leaves are stalked; upper leaves have two lobes clasping the stem. Plants have many white flowers with four petals, giving the plant a white, flat-topped appearance. Heart-shaped seed capsules contain two reddish-brown seeds separated by a narrow partition. Plants emerge in very early spring and have bloomed and set seed by mid-summer.

This perennial is common on alkaline, disturbed soils and is highly competitive with other species once it becomes established. It can be controlled effectively with herbicides. Two other *Cardaria* species, lens-podded whitetop (*C. chalepensis* L.) and hairy whitetop (*C. pubescens* (C.A. Meg) Jarmolenko) are common in the western U.S. with differences in seed capsules and fruit used to identify each species.

Non-standard name: whitetop.

This perennial starts growth very early in the spring.

White flowers with four petals develop into bladder-like seed capsules in mid-summer.

Blue mustard

Chorispora tenella (Pall.) DC.

Blue mustard
Brassicaceae
(Mustard family)

A leafy, somewhat spreading, annual 6 to 18 inches tall, branched mostly from the base. Stems and leaves are sparsely to moderately covered with minute gland-tipped hairs. Leaves are oblanceolate, with wavy or coarsely-toothed margins. Flowers are pale purple, each with 4 petals. Fruits have a conspicuous beak, about 1/3 the length of the pod. Fruits break apart transversely into numerous 2-seeded sections instead of splitting longitudinally as with most mustards.

Blue mustard is considered a native of Russia or southwestern Asia. It inhabits waste areas and cultivated lands, reducing crop yields and affecting crop quality. Blue mustard gives off a disagreeable odor; and dairy animals eating it may produce off-flavor milk. Blue mustard superficially resembles Malcolm stock (*Malcomia africana* (L.) R. Br.), but can be distinguished by globose (rather than stellate) hairs, a conspicuous beak, and 2-seeded fruit segments.

Non-standard name: tenella mustard and purple mustard.

Seedling rosettes of this winter annual mustard have deeply lobed leaves.

This is one of the first plants to flower in early spring. Flowers have 4 petals and are connected with a pedicel to a rough central stem.

225

Flixweed

Descurainia sophia (L.) Webb. ex Prantl

Flixweed and pinnate tansymustard
Brassicaceae
(Mustard family)

Flixweed is a winter annual; 8 to 24 inches high; leaves alternate, 2 to 3 times pinnately compound; segments very narrow or linear; pubescent with branched hairs or nearly glabrous; inflorescence a raceme; petals very small, yellow or greenish-yellow, pod partitioned with 2 to 3 longitudinal nerves, siliques 1/2 to 1 1/4 inches long.

Flixweed was introduced from Europe and is found growing in waste places, fields, roadsides and other disturbed sites. This mustard is distinguished from other mustards because of its finely dissected leaves. Flixweed spreads by seeds from early to late summer.

Pinnate tansymustard, *Descurainia pinnata* (Walt.) Britt, is a winter annual, 4 to 32 inches high; leaves alternate, pinnately dissected; stellate pubescence; inflorescence a raceme; petals yellow or yellowish green to cream; siliques less than 3/4 inch long; pods clavate or linear; two rows of seeds in each seed pod. A native growing in waste places, fields, roadsides, and other disturbed sites. Tansymustard spreads by seeds from early to late summer.

Pinnate tansymustard seed capsules (siliques are less than 3/4 inch long). Pedicels or stems holding seed capsules are nearly the same length as the capsule or longer.

Seedling plants of flixweed and pinnate tansymustard are very similar. Herbicides should be applied at this growth stage or before for effective control.

227

Dyer's woad

Isatis tinctoria L.

Dyer's woad
Brassicaceae
(Mustard family)

Dyer's woad is a winter annual, biennial or short-lived perennial; 12 to 48 inches in height. Leaves of dyer's woad are alternate, simple, petiolate, bluish-green with a whitish nerve on the upper surface of the blade. The inflorescence has a flat top, petals yellow; fruit a pod, indehiscent, black or purplish brown and one-celled, containing a single seed.

Dyer's woad was introduced from Europe. It made its first appearance in the United States in colonial times. It has a thick tap root which may exceed 5 feet in depth. Once leaves are removed mechanically, plants will regenerate from roots. Dyer's woad is first found along roadsides and disturbed sites and spreads from there to rangeland and cropland by seeds from late spring to mid-summer.

Seedling plants appear in the fall and overwinter in this stage. Herbicides are most effectively applied in this growth stage.

Purplish-brown seed pods containing a single seed appear near mid-summer.

229

Perennial pepperweed
Lepidium latifolium L.

Perennial pepperweed
Brassicaceae
(Mustard family)

This plant is a perennial, 1 to over 3 feet in height; leaves lanceolate, bright green to gray-green, entire to toothed, basal leaves larger than upper leaves; inflorescence a raceme. Flowers are white, in dense clusters near ends of branches, very small; fruit a silicle; seeds 2 per fruit, rounded, flattened, slightly hairy, about 1/16 inch long, and reddish-brown.

Perennial pepperweed is a native of southern Europe and western Asia but is now found in many parts of the United States. It has been declared noxious in a number of western states. Deep-seated rootstocks make this weed difficult to control. Perennial pepperweed grows in waste places, wet areas, ditches, roadsides, and cropland. Flowering occurs from early summer to fall.

Non-standard name: broad-leaved peppergrass, tall whitetop, Virginia pepperweed.

Leaves and stems are covered with a waxy layer making this perennial difficult to control.

Dense flower clusters appear in early summer on perennial pepperweed.

Clasping pepperweed
Lepidium perfoliatum L.

Clasping pepperweed
Brassicaceae
(Mustard family)

This weed is a winter annual or annual, 6 to 18 inches tall, stems erect, branched at the top; leaves alternate, of two types, the lower dissected and the upper heart-shaped with a clasping base. Flowers are white to yellow with slender pedicels, in racemes. Fruit a 2-valved orbicular capsule, each containing 2 reddish-brown, somewhat rough, wing-margined seeds about 1/12 inch long.

Clasping pepperweed is a native of Europe and has become established in much of the western U.S. It grows scattered in grain fields, pastures and waste areas. Flowering and seed production occur from April to June.

Upper leaves are heart-shaped, clasping the reddish-brown stems while basal leaves are finely divided.

Each of the oblong capsules contains two reddish-brown seeds. Seeds are formed in early summer from this winter annual.

233

Radish
Raphanus sativus L.

Radish
Brassicaceae
(Mustard family)

An erect branching annual, 2 to 5 feet tall with lower leaves that are pinnately divided, having a large terminal segment and are 1 to 2 inches wide and 3 to 6 inches long. Upper leaves are smaller and mostly undivided with a few small segments. Flowers are 3/4 inch wide and vary from purple to white with petals that are veined with purple to pink. Seed pods are pithy, 1 1/2 to 3 inches long and about 1/4 inch in diameter with 2 to 8 seeds per pod. Seeds are about 1/8 inch long, oval and reddish brown.

Radish is a native of Europe and is widespread in cultivated crops and waste areas in the West. It can be particularly troublesome in cereal crops. Wild radish (*R. raphanistrum* L.) usually has yellow flowers having dark veins.

Flowers showing color variation and distinctly veined petals.

Leaves of seedlings are pinnately divided with large terminal segments.

235

Tumble mustard
Sisymbrium altissimum L.

Tumble mustard
Brassicaceae
(Mustard family)

Tumble mustard is a winter annual or annual, 2 to 5 feet tall; stems simple below, much branched above having a bushy appearance. Leaves alternate and of two types; lower leaves are coarse and divided into broad lobes or leaflets, the upper are much reduced, finer with narrow lobes or segments. Flowers are small, pale yellow, in racemes. Fruit a slender 2-valved capsule 2 to 4 inches long. Seeds are small, numerous, yellow to brown, oblong. They usually have a single groove.

A native of Europe, tumble mustard is now widely scattered throughout the U.S. It is common in small grain fields, rangeland, waste areas and along roadsides. The plant often breaks off at soil level when mature and scatters seed as it tumbles in the wind.

Non-standard name: Jim Hill mustard.

A seedling rosette of this winter annual has leaves similar to the basal leaves of a mature plant, leaves are deeply lobed.

Light yellow, 4-petal flowers are borne at upper stem terminals in early spring.

London rocket
Sisymbrium irio L.

London rocket
Brassicaceae
(Mustard family)

London rocket, a winter annual, is erect, usually 1 1/2 to 2 feet tall. Stems and leaves are smooth. Stems are often branched. Leaves, 1 to 4 inches long, are usually deeply divided with a large terminal lobe. Flowers are small, yellow, and borne on slender stalks in small clusters at the stem tips. As early pods mature, the flowering spikes grow longer; eventually a large number of 1 1/2 to 2 1/2 inch pods are borne along the flowering stem.

The margins of the seedling's first true leaves are always indented, distinguishing seedlings of London rocket from those of shepherdspurse.

London rocket, a European native, is common in irrigated crops, orchards and vineyards. It is also found along roadsides, fence rows, and ditches.

London rocket seedlings have deeply lobed leaves.

Yellow flowers are borne on slender stalks in small clusters.

Field pennycress
Thlaspi arvense L.

Field pennycress
Brassicaceae
(Mustard family)

Field pennycress is an annual; 6 to 18 inches tall; basal leaves lanceolate, simple, entire to lobed, inflorescence a raceme. Petals are white, in clusters on the ends of branches; fruit a pod, circular in outline, obviously winged, rounded, deeply notched at the top, seeds 2 or more in each chamber.

Field pennycress was introduced from Europe. It is a very troublesome weed in grain fields and is also found growing in waste places, roadsides and other disturbed areas. A strong odor is associated with this plant causing dairy animals eating field pennycress to produce a bitter-flavored milk. Field pennycress flowers from late spring to early summer.

Non-standard name: fanweed.

Two seeds are contained in each chamber of this mature pod. They are surrounded by a fan-like structure.

Small white 4-petal flowers are formed in early summer at the ends of branches.

Plains pricklypear
Opuntia polyacantha Haw.

Plains pricklypear
Cactaceae
(Cactus family)

Perennial forming low, spreading, fleshy plants, commonly in clumps but can be erect to 3 feet or more in height, reproducing from stems or seeds. Stems are flat and jointed, spines 4/5 to 1 1/5 inches long, pale or brownish with around 9 per group. Leaves are small and scale-like on young branches, dropping early. Flowers are large; calyx tube does not extend beyond ovary; petals numerous, 1 1/2 to 2 inches long, slightly united; stamens numerous in several rows. The fruit is a pear-shaped berry either juicy or dry, often spiny. Seeds are numerous, 2/10 to 3/10 inch long, white and flattened. There are numerous species of *Opuntia* in the West.

Pricklypear is native, commonly found on dry, sandy soils. It can be troublesome on overgrazed pastures and rangelands. Herbicides effectively control *Opuntia* species.

Individual plains pricklypear may be over 3 feet across with several blooms on the same plant.

Plains pricklypear flowers vary in color from lemon yellow to orange and are waxy in appearance with a green stigma in the center.

Creeping bellflower
Campanula rapunculoides L.

Creeping bellflower
Campanulaceae
(Bluebell family)

A perennial 2 to 4 feet tall spreading by deep-seated creeping roots. The erect stem is often purplish. Leafy plants are slightly hairy to smooth. Leaf blades are somewhat rough and long-ovate to lance-shaped, tapering to the point. Flowers are purple, nodding and bell-shaped, 1 inch or longer.

This is an ornamental plant, frequently escaping from gardens to become a weed problem. Spreading by seeds and creeping rootstocks and thriving in sun or shade are characteristics of this plant, making it a serious weed problem.

Non-standard name: rover bellflower.

Nodding bell-shaped flowers arranged on one side of the flowering stem.

Rough veined ovate leaves allow for easy vegetative identification.

Marijuana
Cannabis sativa L.

Marijuana
Cannabaceae
(Hemp family)

A stout, erect, branching annual, generally 3 to 10 feet tall, having a peculiar odor. Fine hair causes it to be sticky to the touch. The hollow main stem has 4 ridges lengthwise, and produces few branches near the top. Leaves are opposite below and alternate above, compound and palmate with 5 to 10 linear, lance-shaped, pointed leaflets which are deep green on the upper side and light green below, with toothed margins. Both male and female flowers are borne in leaf axils near the top of each plant. Individual plants either have male or female flowers but not both. Male flowers are often borne in loose panicles while female flowers are borne in tighter spikes. The seed is about 1/8 inch long and gray green.

Marijuana is a native of Asia and is considered a controlled substance by law enforcement officials. It contains a resin with narcotic properties. It was introduced in many areas as a crop, used for ropemaking.

Non-standard name: common hemp.

Flowers are borne in leaf axils near the top of the plant.

Palmate leaves with leaflets having toothed margins.

Rocky Mountain beeplant
Cleome serrulata Pursh

Rocky Mountain beeplant
Capparaceae
(Caper family)

Rocky Mountain beeplant is an annual which grows up to 3 feet tall; reproduces by seed; leaves trifoliolate, alternate; flowers numerous, pink or white. Seeds are yellow-brown, 1/8 inch long, borne in a slender pod 1 to 2 inches long. A second species, yellow cleome *(C. lutea* Hook.), has yellow flowers, 5 to 7 palmate leaflets, and is somewhat common in the western United States.

Rocky Mountain beeplant is native to the western region and frequently occupies dry sandy soils along roadsides and waste places. The blossoms are filled with nectar, making it attractive to bees. Indians used the plant for food and making pottery paint. It is undesirable as a forage for livestock due toits unpleasant odor. Because of its showy flowers it is commonly found in gardens.

Capparaceae synonym: Capparidaceae.

Immature plants have pink stems with trifoliolate leaves.

Flowers, containing many showy stamens, appear either white or pink. Seed pods 1 to 2 inches long are attached to the main stem by a slender stalk.

249

Corn cockle
Agrostemma githago L.

Corn cockle
Caryophyllaceae
(Pink family)

A tap-rooted annual with grayish-white hairy foliage and stiff, erect stems growing 1 to 3 feet tall. Leaves are opposite, narrow, stalkless, and 2 to 5 inches long. Flowers are 1/2 inch across and showy. Sepals are hairy and slender, extending well beyond the petals. Petals, five, rose-purple, black-dotted near the base. Petal-tips are notched, broad and rounded. The fruits are about 1/2 inch long, with a toothed opening at the top to allow dissemination of the seeds.

Corn cockle is a native of Europe and has become widely distributed in grainfields, roadsides, and waste areas in some regions of the West.

Flowers have notched petal tips. Slender hairy sepals extend well beyond the petals.

Corn cockle seedling.

Babysbreath

Gypsophila paniculata L.

Babysbreath
Caryophyllaceae
(Pink family)

A perennial with widely branching stems to 3 feet in height. Leaves are in pairs, 3/4 to 4 inches long with sharp points. The inflorescence is diffusely branched, flowers are 1/16 to 1/8 inch wide, with a 5-lobed calyx. Calyx lobes are purple but prominently edged in white; petals are white. The fruit is a small capsule, containing 2 to 5 black seeds, each about 1/12 inch long with a finely pebbled surface.

Babysbreath is an ornamental species that was introduced from Europe and has now escaped cultivation to pastures and rangeland in some areas. Once established, it forms dense stands and is difficult to control. Flowering occurs from June to August.

The small white flowers are useful in floral arrangements.

Narrow, opposite leaves are found along the plant stems.

253

Bouncingbet
Saponaria officinalis L.

Bouncingbet
Caryophyllaceae
(Pink family)

Perennial with stout, erect, smooth, branching stems, up to 3 feet tall, with swollen nodes. Leaves have three distinct veins from the base, are smooth, narrow and 2 to 4 inches long with short petioles. Flowers are conspicuous, and crowded at ends of the main stem and branches, with petals that are generally pink and are slightly notched at the apex.

Introduced from Europe as a garden plant and now escaped and established as a weed in the region. It is poisonous but rarely grazed. However, it spreads rapidly and replaces plants of greater value.

Non-standard name: soapwort.

Opposite leaves originate from slightly swollen nodes.

Flowers with notched petals are crowded at the end of the main stem and branches.

Cone catchfly

Silene conoidea L.

Cone catchfly
Caryophyllaceae
(Pink family)

A simple or branched annual or winter annual 1 to 2 1/2 feet tall. Plants are usually covered with sticky gland-tipped hairs. Leaves are linear, slender, and pointed, opposite, with bases joined on the stem. Flowers have 5 pink, purplish, or white petals with rounded, lightly-toothed margins. The 5-pointed, urn-shaped calyx, with 25 to 30 obvious nerves, inflates up to 3/4 inch wide.

Cone catchfly was introduced from the Old World. It is found in fields, along roadsides, and in other disturbed sites.

Urn-shaped, many-ridged calyx is covered with short sticky hairs.

Cone catchfly seedling.

257

Bladder campion
Silene vulgaris (Moench) Garcke

Bladder campion
Caryophyllaceae
(Pink family)

Perennial with woody rootstocks; stems branching, smooth. Leaves smooth, ovate or lance-shaped, the margins generally not toothed. Flowers are found in clusters at ends of branches, each flower white, and about 1/2 inch wide, on a slender stalk. Calyx at first slender, becoming greatly inflated, thin, veiny, and often purplish as the fruit matures, eventually becoming a veiny, papery sac-like structure surrounding the bulbous fruit. Fruit opens at the toothed top to allow escape of numerous small, grayish, pebbled seeds. White campion (*S. alba* (Mill.) E.H.L. Krause) is an annual or short-lived perennial that is similar but is more or less hairy and dioecious.

Bladder campion was introduced from Europe and has become a serious problem in certain seed crops because the seeds are difficult to separate from crop seeds.

The inflated calyx of bladder campion is slender at the base.

White campion, a similar species, has male (left) and female (right) flowers on different plants, is hairy and the calyx is less inflated.

White campion
Silene alba (Mill.) E.H.L. Krause

White campion
Caryophyllaceae
(Pink family)

White campion is a short-lived perennial or biennial, 1 1/2 to 3 1/2 feet tall. Pointed leaves are opposite and linear, about 3/4 inch wide and 1 to 4 inches long. Flowers, 3/4 inch wide, are borne in open clusters on the ends of plant stems. They have 5 deeply notched, white petals. Fragrant flowers open in the evening but close by noon. Numerous rough seeds are contained by a bulb-like pod about 3/8 inch long.

Sleepy catchfly (*S. antirrhina* L.) looks similar but has downward-pointed hairs on the lower stem with no hairs on upper stems.

Unlike a close relative, bladder campion, it reproduces only by seeds, yet it is often troublesome in cultivated fields. Its seed is difficult to separate from commercially produced clover or alfalfa seed. It is considered a naturalized plant and is common throughout North America and Europe.

Leaves are opposite on main stems and covered with sticky hairs.

Flowers, usually opening in the evening, are located on ends of stems.

261

Corn spurry
Spergula arvensis L.

Corn spurry
Caryophyllaceae
(Pink family)

An annual that is much branched at the base, the branches 1/2 to 2 feet long, somewhat sticky, erect or more or less spreading. Leaves are narrow, cord-like and fleshy, arranged in a series of apparent whorls at the nodes. Flowers, less than 1/4 inch wide, are white, and in loose clusters at ends of the branches. Fruit, 1/4 inch long, contain seeds that are somewhat flattened, dull black, usually with minute whitish warts and a circular whitish wing.

Naturalized from Europe, corn spurry is found in the Pacific Northwest states, Colorado and Wyoming.

Non-standard names: stickwort and starwort.

Stems with whorls of slender fleshy leaves.

White, terminal flowers less than 1/4 inch wide of corn spurry.

263

Common chickweed
Stellaria media (L.) Vill.

Common chickweed
Caryophyllaceae
(Pink family)

Annual or winter annual reproducing by seeds and creeping stems that root at the nodes. Stems with numerous branches and a conspicuous line of hairs on one side, are sometimes ascending but commonly prostrate, forming mats of plants 4 to 12 inches high. Leaves up to 1 1/2 inches long, upper leaves without petioles, lower petioled and often hairy toward base or on petiole. Flowers about 1/4 inch across, white, with petals deeply 2-parted, shorter than sepals.

Several chickweeds in the genus *Cerastium* are found world-wide and differ from common chickweed in being more or less hairy all over. Field chickweed (*C. arvense* L.) and mouseear chickweed (*C. vulgatum* L.) are perennials. Sticky chickweed (*C. viscosum* L., also called *C. glomeratum* Thuill.) is an annual.

Chickweeds are weedy in fields, also gardens, lawns, and ornamental plantings.

The hairy leaf may vary in size but is typical of the chickweeds in the genus Cerastium.

Note the deeply notched petals that are typical of the chickweeds.

Cowcockle
Vaccaria pyramidata Medic.

Cowcockle
Caryophyllaceae
(Pink family)

A gray-green, tap-rooted, annual growing 1 1/2 to 3 feet tall. Stems are much-branched, with each branch ending in a flower. Leaves are smooth, narrow to broad, lance-shaped, opposite, and somewhat clasping around the stem. Flowers are small, but conspicuous, with 5 toothed pink or red petals. The smooth inflated calyx is strongly 5-angled, with green or purplish veins. Fruits remain in the calyx at maturity. Seeds are gray with a pebbled surface.

Cowcockle is a European weed that inhabits foothills, roadsides, waste areas, and cropland. The seeds are poisonous to livestock.

Synonyms include: *V. segetalis* (Neck.) Garcke ex Asch., *Saponaria vaccaria* L.

Non-standard name: cowherb.

Flower petals are pink with a notched tip. The calyx is smooth and strongly 5-angled when viewed in cross section.

Cowcockle seedling showing typical lance-shaped leaves.

Netseed lambsquarters
Chenopodium berlandieri Moq.

Netseed lambsquarters
Chenopodiaceae
(Goosefoot family)

Extremely variable annual, 1 to 6 feet tall, stems erect, much branched and often striped with pink or purple; leaves alternate, the lower often wavy margined to somewhat lobed, the upper narrower and often entire, undersurface white to grayish-mealy. Flowers are small, inconspicuous, greenish-gray, mealy, crowded in axils and at tips and branches of stem, calyx strongly keeled, seeds numerous, dark gray to black with a honey-combed surface.

Netseed lambsquarters is common in cultivated fields, gardens, and waste areas. It is a very competitive weed because of its rapid growth and high water use. Lambsquarters also serves as a host for the beet leafhopper which transmits curly top virus to sugarbeets. Netseed lambsquarters is often eaten in salad or as greens when the plant is young and tender. Flowering and seed production may occur from July to September. Common lambs-quarters, *C. album* L., a native of Europe, has become established throughout most of North America. It can be distinguished by its shiny black seeds and its calyx is not keeled.

Seedling with leaves having tiny silver scales on the leaf surface.

Flowers are inconspicuous and appear as mealy structures in leaf axils and along the terminal stem.

269

Nettleleaf goosefoot
Chenopodium murale L.

Nettleleaf goosefoot
Chenopodiaceae
(Goosefoot family)

A bushy annual 1 to 3 feet high with stems that are erect or lateral and then erect. The leaves are 1 to 2 inches long, alternate, pointed at the tip with 1 to 8 irregular teeth along each margin, having the general outline of a "goose's foot." The upper surface of the leaf is dark green while the lower surface and younger plant parts have a lighter mealy appearance. Flowers are small and greenish, borne in dense axillary or terminal spike-like panicles. Seeds are tiny, dull black and disc-shaped, enclosed by a thin papery fruit wall and about 1/18 inch across.

Nettleleaf goosefoot was introduced from Europe and is now widespread throughout the United States and southern Canada. It is a common weed in cultivated fields, gardens and waste areas.

Dark green, shiny goosefoot-shaped leaves of a seedling plant.

Small, greenish flowers are borne in a dense terminal inflorescence.

271

Halogeton
Halogeton glomeratus (Stephen ex Bieb.) C.A. Mey.

Halogeton
Chenopodiaceae
(Goosefoot family)

An annual weed ranging in height from a few inches to over 18 inches. Main stems branch from the base, spreading at first, and then becoming erect. Plants are blue-green in the spring and early summer, turning red or yellow by late summer. Leaves are small, fleshy, and nearly tubular, ending abruptly, tipped with a delicate needle-like spine. Flowers are green and inconspicuous, borne in leaf axils. Plants resemble Russian thistle in early stages but they can be distinguished by leaf shape, and by the presence of minute cottony hairs in the leaf axils.

Halogeton is a native of Asia that has rapidly invaded millions of acres in the western states. It seems ideally adapted to the alkaline soils and semi-arid environment of high-desert winter livestock ranges. Halogeton is not an extremely competitive plant, but it readily invades disturbed or over-grazed lands. It is usually most concentrated along roadsides, sheep trails and near areas where livestock congregate. The plant produces toxic oxalates that are especially poisonous to sheep, though cattle may also be affected. Halogeton is readily grazed at times, and is responsible for thousands of livestock poisonings.

Fleshy leaves terminating with a needle-like structure are connected to a red colored stem.

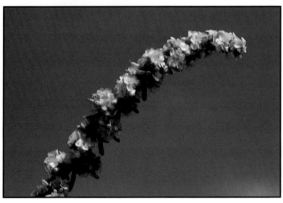

Green flowers borne in leaf axils in the fall surround each plant stem.

Kochia
Kochia scoparia (L.) Schrad.

Kochia
Chenopodiaceae
(Goosefoot family)

Annual, 1 to 6 feet tall, stems much branched, round, slender, usually soft-hairy, but occasionally smooth, often red-tinged. Leaves alternate, lance-shaped, entire 1/2 to 2 inches long, margins fringed with hairs; the upper surface is usually smooth, the lower surface usually covered with soft hairs; leaf blades with 3 or 5 prominent veins. Flowers are inconspicuous, sessile in the axils of upper leaves and form short, dense, bracted spikes. Seed wedge-shaped, dull brown, slightly ribbed and approximately 1/16 inch long.

Native of Asia, introduced from Europe, kochia has escaped from cultivation as an ornamental and is now found throughout North America. It is common in cultivated fields, gardens, roadsides, ditchbanks and waste areas throughout the western U.S. While it is usually considered an objectionable weed, kochia is readily grazed by livestock. It sometimes contains high nitrate levels and can be toxic. Flowering and seed production may occur from July to October.

Five-hook bassia (*Bassia hyssopifolia* (Pall.) Kuntze), is easily distinguished from kochia by the 5 hooked structures on each seed.

Seedlings of kochia emerge in very early spring and should be treated with herbicides in this stage.

Flowers are inconspicuous, forming dense spikes in leaf axils.

275

Russian thistle

Salsola iberica Sennen

Russian thistle
Chenopodiaceae
(Goosefoot family)

A rounded, bushy, much branched annual, 1/2 to 3 feet tall, reproducing by seed. Stems are usually red or purple striped. Leaves are alternate; the first are long, string-like and soft, with later leaves short, scale-like and tipped with a stiff spine. Inconspicuous green flowers are borne in axils of upper leaves, each flower accompanied by a pair of spiny bracts.

Seeds are spread as mature plants break off at ground level and are scattered by the wind as tumbleweeds. Rapid germination and seedling establishment occur after only brief and limited amounts of precipitation. Since Russian thistle was introduced (from Russia) in the late 1800s, it has become one of the most common and troublesome weeds in the drier regions of the U.S. It is well adapted to cultivated dryland agriculture, but is also found on disturbed wastelands, over-grazed rangeland, and even some irrigated cropland. Barbwire Russian thistle (*S. paulsenii* Litv.) is similar in overall appearance but is generally more coarse and robust, with broader and more rigid spine-tipped leaves.

Russian thistle synonyms include: *S. kali* L., *S. kali* L. var. *tenuifolia* Tausch, *S. kali* L. var. *ruthenica* (Iljin) Soo, and *S. pesitfer* A. Nels.

Seedling plants have long, fleshy leaves; herbicide applications should be made at this growth stage or before.

Stems are striped with purple at most growth stages. Flowers are found in leaf axils at maturity.

Greasewood
Sarcobatus vermiculatus (Hook.) Torr.

Greasewood
Chenopodiaceae
(Goosefoot family)

A native perennial shrub becoming a dominant species on saline or alkaline flood plains. This woody species has rigid stems that are white to gray, growing over 7 feet tall. Linear round leaves are pale green, usually less than 1 inch long and attached without a petiole to a woody stem. Flowers appearing in late summer are yellow, inconspicuous, with female flowers located below male flowers on the same plant. The plant starts growth in early spring and loses its leaves after frost.

Greasewood is a moderately poisonous plant if consumed in large amounts by sheep and cattle. Sheep are often poisoned in the fall from eating large amounts of fallen leaves. Toxicity increases as the plants mature. Leaves contain oxalates of potassium and sodium which cause death of livestock in 4 to 6 hours after they have been consumed. Sheep may die after eating up to 2 pounds of leaves while cattle need to consume 3 to 4 pounds for death to occur. Commonly used herbicides defoliate plants but they usually resprout, causing greasewood to be a difficult species to control.

Young greasewood plants have fleshy leaves that are individually connected to white woody stems.

In late summer, flowers appear inconspicuously.

Common St. Johnswort
Hypericum perforatum L.

Common St. Johnswort
Clusiaceae
(St. Johnswort family)

A perennial reproducing by seeds or short runners. Stems are 1 to 3 feet high, erect, with numerous branches, somewhat 2-ridged, rust-colored, woody at their base. Leaves are opposite, sessile, entire, elliptic to oblong, not over 1 inch long, covered with transparent dots. Flowers are 3/4 inch in diameter, bright yellow, numerous in flat-topped cymes, with 5 separate petals with occasional minute black dots around the edges. Petals are twice as long as the sepals. Stamens are numerous, arranged in 3 groups. Seed pods are 1/4 inch long, rust-brown, 3-celled capsules, each with numerous seeds.

St. Johnswort, originally from Europe, is frequently found in the Pacific Northwest, often on sandy or gravelly soils. The weed contains a toxic substance which affects white-haired animals. Affected animals rarely die, but will often lose weight and develop a skin irritation when exposed to strong sunlight. St. Johnswort is an abundant weed in Australia where research has identified three insect species native to Europe which selectively feed on the plant. Insects introduced to the western United States and Canada have provided partial control of the weed.

Clusiaceae synonym: Hypericaceae.

Leaves of St. Johnswort are oval in shape with prominent veins. Tiny transparent dots are visible when leaves are held up to a light source.

Yellow flowers with 5 petals and many stamens appear in early summer.

281

Hedge bindweed
Calystegia sepium (L.) R. Br.

Hedge bindweed
Convolvulaceae
(Morningglory family)

Perennial from elongated rhizomes with stems trailing or climbing, up to 9 feet or more in length. Leaves are alternate, long-stalked, the leaf blades 1 to 5 inches long, and generally heart-shaped with basal lobes that are rounded or variously angled but do not flare out. Flowers are generally solitary in the leaf axils, trumpet-shaped, white to deep pink, and 1 to 3 inches long. The fruit are nearly round, about 3/8 inch long, splitting at maturity to release 2 to 4 seeds. Seeds are dull gray to brown or black and minutely roughened.

Hedge bindweed is native to the eastern U.S., but is now widely distributed. It presents problems in fence rows and ornamental planting where it climbs and spreads over shrubbery and other ornamentals and is difficult to control.

Hedge bindweed synonym: *Convolvulus sepium* L.

Non-standard names: lady's nightcap, bell-bind and Rutland beauty.

Two large bracts enclosing the base of the flower distinguish this species from field bindweed which has 2 minute bracts further down the flower stem.

Cotyledon leaves of hedge bindweed.

Field bindweed
Convolvulus arvensis L.

Field bindweed
Convolvulaceae
(Morningglory family)

Field bindweed is a perennial from an extensive root system, often climbing or forming dense tangled mats. Stems are prostrate, 1 to 4 feet long. Leaves alternate, more or less arrowhead-shaped, pointed or blunt lobes at the base. The flowers are bell- or trumpet-shaped, white to pinkish, approximately 1 inch in diameter with 2 small bracts located 1 inch below the flower. Fruit is a small, round capsule, usually 4-seeded.

Field bindweed was introduced from Europe and has become a widespread and serious weed problem in all parts of the U.S. except the southeastern states. In the western United States, it is extensively distributed in cultivated fields and waste places. Because of its remarkable adaptability to different environmental conditions, it may be found at altitudes as high as 10,000 feet. It is a difficult weed to eradicate because of the long, deep taproot which can penetrate the soil to a depth of 10 feet and which gives rise to numerous long lateral roots. Seeds remain viable for up to 50 years. The flowering period is from late June until frost in the fall.

Non-standard names: creeping Jenny, morningglory, perennial morningglory.

Leaves of field bindweed are shaped like arrowheads. They are normally slender with sharp pointed lobes, though many variations occur.

Flowers are funnel-shaped and vary in color from white to pink. Note tiny bracts 1 inch below base of flower.

285

Field dodder
Cuscuta campestris Yuncker

Field dodder
Convolvulaceae
(Morningglory family)

This parasitic annual lacks chlorophyll. Stems are yellowish, thread-like and twining, leaves are reduced to thread-like scales. Flowers are numerous in compact clusters, 5-parted and shallowly cupped, white to pink. Fruit is a 2- to 4-seeded globular capsule which is somewhat depressed on the top. Seeds are small, oval, gray to red and 1/25 inch in length.

Dodder is widely distributed over much of the U.S. with several species present in the western United States. Largeseed dodder (*C. indecora* Choisy) and field dodder (*C. campestris* Yuncker) are the major problem species in the West. Dodder seeds germinate on the soil surface and the resulting plant develops a small root system and 2- to 4-inch long thread-like stalk which attaches to green plants. Once attached, the root system disappears and the dodder becomes wholly parasitic. Many broadleaf plants serve as hosts for this parasite, but alfalfa and clover are especially susceptible. Dodder seeds are fairly long-lived in the soil and infestation may occur in areas where host plants were not grown for several years. Flowering period is July to October.

Seeds of field dodder germinate in early spring and seedlings quickly attach to host plants to obtain food supplies.

This parasitic annual attaches to alfalfa and produces clusters of flowers in late summer.

287

Red morningglory
Ipomoea coccinea L.

Red morningglory
Convolvulaceae
(Morningglory family)

Red morningglory is a vining or twining hairless annual with reddish, ridged stems. Leaves are alternate, on petioles 1 to 4 inches long, with 2 principle shapes. On some plants the leaves are unlobed with a heart-shaped base, usually 1 1/2 to 2 1/2 inches long, and conspicuously long-pointed. On other plants, some or all of the leaves are deeply cut into 3 to 5 finger-like lobes. Flowers are scarlet red and narrowly trumpet-shaped, 1 to 1 1/4 inches long. Two to several flowers are borne on a 3- to 5-inch stalk arising from the leaf axils. The globe-shaped seedpod is plump, somewhat egg-shaped, but angular, and about 1/8 inch long.

Red morningglory is native in the southwestern United States and tropical America.

Non-standard names: scarlet morningglory, starglory.

The leaf shape of red morningglory varies from unlobed to multi-lobed.

Flowers of red morningglory are narrowly trumpet-shaped and scarlet red in color.

Ivyleaf morningglory
Ipomoea hederacea (L.) Jacq.

Ivyleaf morningglory
Convolvulaceae
(Morningglory family)

A trailing annual from a taproot, with stems up to 20 feet long. The entire plant is hairy. Leaves vary in shape, each on 2- to 4-inch long petioles. Some are heart-shaped, looking very similar to the leaves of tall morningglory (*I. purpurea* (L.) Roth, p. 292) which has a uniform leaf shape on the entire plant. Others vary from barely angular to 3-lobed, to very deeply 3-lobed, 1 1/2 to 4 inches long, with conspicuously heart-shaped bases. A few leaves even have 5 finger-like lobes. Flowers are blue, purple, or whitish, 1 to 1 3/4 inches long, and in clusters of 1 to 5. The 5-lobed calyx is conspicuously hairy at the base, 1/3 to 1/2 inch long and can be 1 inch in length. The globe-shaped seedpod is yellowish and contains 4 seeds.

Native of tropical America, woolly morningglory can be found throughout the southwestern states.

Non-standard name: Mexican morningglory.

Leaves are 3-lobed, but have variations which range from heart-shaped to 5-lobed.

Flowers are blue, purple, or even white, opening in the morning and closing in the evening.

Tall morningglory
Ipomoea purpurea (L.) Roth

Tall morningglory
Convolvulaceae
(Morningglory family)

This climbing and twining, annual morningglory comes from a fibrous root system, unlike ivyleaf morningglory (*I. hederacea*, p. 290) which has a taproot. Stem length varies from 5 to 13 feet. It has leaves similar to woolly morningglory except all the leaves of tall morningglory are heart-shaped and unlobed, more or less hairy, and pointed at the tip. Flowers are similar to woolly morningglory but are often larger. Color varies from white to blue, or purple to bright pink. The calyx is conspicuously hairy and 1/2 to 3/4 inch long. The globe-shaped seedpods are similar to red morningglory (*I. coccinea* L.).

Tall morningglory is a native of tropical America. It, along with red and woolly morningglory, is commonly found in the Southwest.

Tall morningglory seedlings have heart-shaped leaves.

Purple-blue flowers look similar to woolly morningglory but heart-shaped leaves are uniform throughout the plant.

Ivy gourd
Coccinia grandis (L.) Voigt

Ivy gourd
Cucurbitaceae
(Cucumber family)

Ivy gourd is a climbing perennial with tendrils and a tuberous root system. Leaves are simple, up to 4 inches wide and long and can vary from being several-angled to deeply palmately lobed. Flowers are white, and dioecious. Mature fruits contain numerous seeds, are red, oblong, and 2 to 3 inches long.

Probably introduced as an ornamental, ivy gourd is a vigorous vine that is found in Hawaii throughout the lowlands of the island of Oahu, and in the Kona District on the island of Hawaii. It climbs over shrubs and trees, forming a dense, sun-blocking canopy. Because of this close association with other plants, chemical control is difficult. Seed dispersal is attributed to birds that feed on the red fruits. Ivy gourd is reportedly used for food or medicinal purposes in southeast Asia and India.

Several-angled leaves up to 4 inches long and wide and flowers up to 3 inches long are formed on ivy gourd.

Oblong fruits contain many seeds and often plants have tendrils.

Western wildcucumber

Marah oreganus (T. & G.) T.J. Howell

Western wildcucumber
Cucurbitaceae
(Gourd family)

A perennial regenerating from an enormous taproot. The stem is long, thick, angled, and trailing or climbing. Leaves are stalked, blades lobed, roughened, and sometimes reaching 6 inches or more in length and width. Flowers are waxy-white and somewhat star-shaped. The fruit is gourd-like, several inches long, beaked at the apex, fleshy at first and somewhat spiny.

Wildcucumber is native to the western U.S. and Canada. It occurs along roadsides and fence rows as well as in open fields and waste areas.

Synonym: *Echinocystis oregana* Cogn.

Non-standard names: bigroot, manroot, old-man-in-the-ground.

Gourd-like spiny fruit and small star-shaped flowers are good identification characteristics.

Storage roots on wildcucumber can attain great size.

297

Yellow nutsedge
Cyperus esculentus L.

Yellow nutsedge
Cyperaceae
(Sedge family)

Yellow nutsedge is an aggressive perennial superficially resembling a grass. Plants range from 6 to 30 inches tall, with 3-ranked leaves, and 3-angled (triangular in cross section) pithy stems. True leaves originate from the base of each stem, while long leaf-like bracts radiate out from a common point just below the umbrella-like flower cluster; otherwise, stems are naked. Leaves and stems have a waxy or shiny appearance. Spikelets are yellowish-brown, and are borne on the ends of several to many slender branches of unequal length. Yellow nutsedge can spread by seed, creeping rootstocks, or by small underground nutlets. The many hard brown nutlets (1/2 to 3/4 inch long) may lie dormant in the soil for several years before producing new plants.

Yellow nutsedge was probably introduced from the Old World, and has now invaded cultivated agricultural lands throughout North America. It prefers moist soils, becoming most troublesome in potatoes, beans, corn, gardens and ornamentals. *Cyperus* is a genus of some 600 species, but yellow and purple nutsedge are the primary weedy sedges in our region.

Immature plants have 3-ranked leaves, a characteristic unlike grasses which are 2-ranked.

Underground nutlets often propagate new plants in cultivated areas.

Purple nutsedge
Cyperus rotundus L.

Purple nutsedge
Cyperaceae
(Sedge family)

A spreading perennial with upright stems 1 to 2 feet high. Leaves are 3-ranked and grass-like, 1/8 to 1/3 inch wide and 2 to 6 inches in length. Flower stems are 3-cornered and generally longer than the basal leaves. Leaf-like bracts subtending the inflorescence are shorter than the inflorescence itself which consists of numerous purplish spikelets. The underground tubers or nutlets are oblong and covered by persistent reddish scales and are often formed in chains while tubers of yellow nutsedge (*C. esculentus* L.) are almost smooth, rounder and are usually formed at the tip of numerous rhizomes.

Purple nutsedge was imported from Europe and thrives in moist conditions in sandy soil. It is commonly found in Arizona and southern California, in turf, ornamental areas, cultivated fields and ditch banks.

Non-standard names: nutgrass, yellow nutgrass.

Inflorescence of purple nutsedge (left) has subtending leaf-like bracts which are shorter than the inflorescence itself. Yellow nutsedge with its longer subtending bracts is pictured right.

Tubers and subsequently generated new plants of purple nutsedge are formed in chains (left). Yellow nutsedge tubers are larger and formed at the end of numerous rhizomes (right).

301

Common teasel
Dipsacus fullonum L.

Common teasel
Dipsacaceae
(Teasel family)

Common teasel is a stout, taprooted biennial which grows to 6 feet tall, branched above. The stem is striate-angled with several rows of downward turned prickles. Leaves are conspicuously veined, with stiff prickles on the lower midrib. The basal rosette of leaves usually dies early in the second season. Stem leaves lanceolate up to 10 inches long, the opposite leaves of the stem have fused bases which trap rain water. Flowers are purple, borne in dense heads, each flower subtended by spine-like bractlets. Corolla is 4-lobed. Involucral bracts at the base of the head are generally longer than the head. Fruits are 4-angled, each with a single seed.

Common teasel is a native of Europe, now widespread as a weed in North America. It is spreading rapidly in the Pacific Northwest, in moist sites, especially along irrigation ditches, canals and disturbed sites. In the fall the stems and fruiting heads are commonly silvered or gilded for winter bouquets. Flowering occurs from July to August.

Non-standard name: teasel.

Teasel is a biennial plant producing a rosette the first year. It has a wrinkled appearance and spines on the lower midrib of the leaf.

In the second year of the growth cycle, teasel produces spiny heads often reaching lengths over 2 inches. Purple flowers are protected by spine-like bractlets.

Russian-olive
Elaeagnus angustifolia L.

Russian-olive
Elaeagnaceae
(Oleaster family)

A fast-growing tree of moderate size, normally reaching heights from 10 to 25 feet. Trunks and branches are armed with 1- to 2-inch woody thorns. Leaves are narrow, 2 to 3 inches long, and covered with minute scales which give the foliage a distinctive silvery appearance. Scales are usually more abundant on the underside of leaves. Flowers are yellow, and arranged in clusters. Fruits, shaped like small olives, are silvery when first formed, but turn tan to brown at maturity.

Introduced from Europe, Russian-olive is promoted as a desirable ornamental shade tree, and is recognized as a source of food and protection for wildlife. However, when allowed to invade low-lying pastures, meadows, or waterways it can become a serious weed problem.

Leaves are silvery, especially on the lower surface. Woody stems are often reddish brown.

Stems have stiff woody thorns. Fruits resemble small tan or silvery olives.

Field horsetail
Equisetum arvense L.

Field horsetail
Equisetaceae
(Horsetail family)

A perennial with aerial stems and underground tuber-bearing rootstocks. Field horsetail has dimorphic stems: a fertile cone-bearing stem which arises in early spring is flesh-colored and 1/2 to 1 foot tall with cones 3/4 to 1 1/2 inches long; a sterile or vegetative stem arises after the fertile stem and is 1 1/5 to 2 feet tall with many whorls of slender, green jointed branches. Giant horsetail (*E. telmateia* Ehrh.) resembles field horsetail but is much more robust with sterile stems over 1 1/2 feet high and cones which are 1 1/2 to 4 inches long.

Both species are native and common in areas with high water tables.

Tall, robust sterile stems of giant horsetail.

Green, tall sterile stems and shorter cone-bearing fertile stems of giant horsetail.

Smooth scouringrush
Equisetum laevigatum A.

Smooth scouringrush
Equisetaceae
(Horsetail family)

A tenacious perennial plant with deep, spreading rootstocks. Stems are rough (high silica content), jointed and hollow. Leaves are scale-like appendages located at stem nodes. Fertile stems have a terminal spore-producing cone. Several species of *Equisetum* are found in the West, including field horsetail (*E. arvense* L.), and scouringrush (*E. hyemale* L.). Field horsetail produces whorls of branches at each stem node while scouringrush is coarse with evergreen stems and very apparent bands at the base of each collar.

Field horsetail is adapted to wet areas, while scouringrush can be found either along streambanks and or in relatively dry soils. *Equisetum* can create serious maintenance problems along highway rights-of-way and irrigation waterways; and is difficult to control in cropland. At least some species within this genus are poisonous to livestock, affecting primarily horses and cattle.

Reproductive spore producing cones develop in July and August.

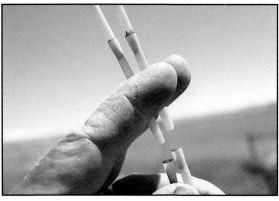

Rigid hollow stems are segmented and are easily pulled apart at nodes.

309

Turkey mullein
Eremocarpus setigerus (Hook.) Benth.

Turkey mullein
Euphorbiaceae
(Spurge family)

A grayish-green, spreading or prostrate annual, branching from the base. A single plant may cover an area from 3 inches to 2 feet in diameter. The leaves are thick and broadly ovate to rounded, with 3 main veins from the base. The entire plant surface is covered by a thick gray layer of minute star-shaped hairs. Flowers are inconspicuous, of 2 kinds, borne in the lower leaf axils and at the ends of branches.

Turkey mullein is a native of the Pacific coast and is found east to Nevada. It thrives on dry sandy soils. The hairy covering of the stems and leaves is as irritating to many persons as poison oak.

Flowers are borne in the lower leaf axils and at the ends of branches.

The entire plant is covered with a thick gray layer of hairs.

Ridgeseed spurge
Euphorbia glyptosperma Engelm.

Ridgeseed spurge
Euphorbiaceae
(Spurge family)

Prostrate annuals, often forming a dense mat, with dark green opposite leaves, 1/8 to 1/2 inch long and 1/8 inch wide. Stems exude a milky latex juice when broken. The tiny pinkish flowers consist only of stamens and pistils and are grouped into small flower-like clusters in the leaf axils. The 3-lobed seedpods are 1/16 inch or less long. The oblong seeds are about 1/25 inch long.

There are three commonly found species in the western United States. Spotted spurge (*E. maculata* L.) has hairy stems and leaves with a large purple spot on each leaf. Ground spurge (*E. prostrata* Ait.) has hairy stems and leaves but no purple spot. Ridgeseed spurge (*E. glyptosperma* Engelm.) has entire leaf margins with smooth stems and leaves and seeds which are coarsely transcorrugated.

Spotted spurge has a purple spot on each leaf. All prostrate spurge plants contain milky juice as shown.

Tiny pinkish flowers are grouped into clusters in the leaf axils.

313

Toothed spurge
Euphorbia dentata Michx.

Toothed spurge
Euphorbiaceae
(Spurge family)

This native annual species is found from New York to Arizona. Stems are erect or curve upward, 8 to 24 inches tall, with branches that also curve upward. Leaves are opposite (lower ones sometimes alternate), 1/2 to 3 inches long, ovate to lance-shaped, usually hairy, with prominent veins on the undersides, often with a central dark reddish spot; margins are coarsely toothed. Flowers are small, without petals, and occur in clusters at the ends of shoots and branches. Seed capsules are 3-celled, smooth, yellow-green to green, and normally produce 3 seeds. Seeds are spherical and egg-shaped, inconspicuously 4-angled, tuberculate, gray, and about 1/6 inch long. White, milky juice is found in all plant parts.

Toothed spurge grows well in dry or moist soils. Habitats include roadsides, waste areas, gardens, and cultivated fields, particularly spring-planted crops.

Seeds are contained in 3-valved capsules and leaves are often blotched with red markings.

Upper leaves are opposite with lower ones sometimes alternate. Stems contain a milky juice.

Leafy spurge
Euphorbia esula L.

Leafy spurge
Euphorbiaceae
(Spurge family)

Perennial, up to 3 feet tall; reproduces by vigorous rootstalks and seed. Leaves are alternate, narrow, 1 to 4 inches long. Stems are thickly clustered. Flowers are yellowish-green, small, arranged in numerous small clusters and subtended by paired heart-shaped yellow-green bracts. Roots are brown, containing numerous pink buds which may produce new shoots or roots. The entire plant contains a milky juice. Seeds are oblong, grayish to purple, contained in a 3-celled capsule, each cell containing a single seed.

Leafy spurge is native to Eurasia and was brought into the United States as a seed impurity about 1827. However, it seems to be a serious problem only in North America where it infests almost 2.5 million acres, mostly in southern Canada and the northcentral United States. It has been reported to cause severe irritation of the mouth and digestive tract in cattle which may result in death. Capsules explode when dry, often projecting seeds as far as 15 feet. Seeds may be viable in the soil for at least 8 years. An extensive root system containing large nutrient reserves makes leafy spurge extremely difficult to control.

Heart-shaped yellow bracts surround the 3-celled seed capsule, each cell containing a single seed.

Pink buds which form new shoots are common on leafy spurge crowns, and roots. Rooting depths of over 14 feet are reported with this prolific species.

Castorbean

Ricinus communis L.

Castorbean
Euphorbiaceae
(Spurge family)

A tall, stout annual herb 4 to 6 feet in height. Leaves, large, palmately-lobed with 5 to 22 lobes with serrated leaf margins, having petioles with conspicuous glands. The flowers are borne in racemes or panicled clusters having female flowers above the male flowers. Each fruit contains up to 3 seeds, borne in a round spiny fruit that is often reddish. Seeds are smooth and bean-shaped, often variously marked and colored.

Castorbean is a cultivated oil crop which escapes to ditchbanks, roadsides and waste areas. It has caused poisoning in animals and humans. Skin irritation may result from handling seeds which are also highly toxic when eaten.

Spiny fruits grow in clusters, each containing up to 3 seeds.

Poisonous seeds are smooth and bean-shaped with a mottled appearance.

319

Camelthorn
Alhagi pseudalhagi (Bieb.) Desv.

Camelthorn
Fabaceae
(Pea family)

Camelthorn is a spiny, intricately branched, perennial shrub 1 1/2 to 4 feet tall. Reproduction is by seed and deep vertical and horizontal roots and rhizomes branching extensively at depths of 2 to 4 feet. The greenish stems are striate, glabrous, with slender spines 1/4 to 1 3/4 inches long. Single leaves are alternate, wedge-shaped, hairless on the upper surface, with hairs on the underside. They are 1/4 to 1 1/4 inches long and 1/8 to 1/2 inch wide. Flowers are small, pea-like, pinkish purple to maroon, occurring on short spine-tipped branches along the upper portion of the plant. The reddish-brown jointed seedpods are curved upward, deeply indented, with each seed being clearly outlined in the pod.

Camelthorn was introduced from Asia and grows well on dry or moist sites. It is now reported in the southwestern U.S. as well as Washington, and has been reported to spread rapidly along streams and canals. Also called *A. camelorum* Fisch.

Spines, 1/4 to 1 3/4 inches long, with yellow tips, are arranged along plant stems.

Flowers are pea-like, 3/8 inch long, pinkish purple to maroon.

Twogrooved milkvetch
Astragalus bisulcatus (Hook.) Gray

Twogrooved milkvetch
Fabaceae
(Pea family)

Twogrooved milkvetch is a perennial upright herb growing up to 30 inches tall. Stems are dark purple as plants mature. Opposite, paired, hairy leaflets, oblong in shape, vary in numbers but generally are from 11 to 30 per leaf. Flowers are generally purple, sometimes blue or white, clustered near the end of plant branches. Fruit is a pod having two parallel rounded grooves. Plants are indicators of saline soils and often have a strong selenium odor.

Members of this genus are poisonous, affecting cattle, sheep, and horses. Plants are poisonous throughout the growing season, containing glucosides that cause respiratory problems and paralysis of the hind legs in livestock. As little as 2 pounds can cause acute poisoning in mature cows within a few hours after being eaten. Animals often seek out plants, and have become addicted to milkvetches once they graze them. Moving affected livestock to non-infested areas will reduce losses. Members of this genus can be controlled with herbicides before plants reach full bloom.

Seed formation takes place in pods with two grooves running parallel down each pod. Stems are purple.

Purple or blue flowers cluster at terminal ends of branches in early summer.

323

Scotch broom
Cytisus scoparius (L.) Link

Scotch broom
Fabaceae
(Pea family)

A woody shrub, up to 10 feet tall with many more-or-less erect branches that are angled and dark green. Leaves are mostly 3-parted with entire leaflets. Flowers are showy, yellow and abundant. Pods are flattened, brown or black, with white hair on the margins.

Scotch broom is a widespread pest of the Pacific coast, where it was introduced as an ornamental. This aggressive shrub is a problem in pastures, forests and wasteland. There are several weedy species of the genus *Cytisus* that are found on the Pacific coast. The seeds remain viable in the soil for many years.

The pods at maturity can split noisily, ejecting the seeds some distance from the plant.

The showy yellow legume flowers illustrate why this plant was first introduced as an ornamental.

Goatsrue
Galega officinalis L.

Goatsrue
Fabaceae
(Pea family)

A taprooted perennial legume, growing 2 to 5 feet tall, reproducing by seed. Leaves are odd-pinnate with 5 to 8 pairs of leaflets. Flowers are purple, blue or white, borne in terminal and axillary racemes. Pods are narrow, round in cross section, and slightly more than 1 inch long.

Goatsrue was intentionally introduced from the Middle East as a potential livestock forage, but was found to be unpalatable and highly toxic. It was allowed to escape, eventually spreading into cropland, waterways, pastures, fencelines, roadways, and marshy areas. Goatsrue seeds are spread primarily in irrigation water; but have also been known to move in contaminated harvest equipment, soil-moving equipment, animal manure, or alfalfa seed. Goatsrue has recently been the object of an intensive federal eradication program, and now is known to infest only a single county in northern Utah.

Seedpods are narrow, round in cross section and slightly more than 1 inch long.

Flowers appear at stem terminals and range in color from blue, purple or white.

Wild licorice
Glycyrrhiza lepidota (Nutt.) Pursh

Wild licorice
Fabaceae
(Pea family)

Wild licorice is a perennial reproducing from deep, spreading roots or seeds. Stems 1 to 3 feet tall, erect, simple or with upper part producing erect branches. Leaves alternate, pinnately compound with 11 to 19 deeply veined lanceolate leaflets with glandular dots when mature. Flowers in short axillary spikes on long peduncles; calyx with 2 upper teeth shorter and partly united; corolla with narrow standard and blunt keel, green-white to white, stamens – 9 fused by filaments and 1 separate. Seed pod about 1/2 to 3/4 inch long, burlike, covered with stout, hooked prickles; seeds to 1/10 inch long, bean-shaped, reddish-brown, smooth and dull.

Wild licorice is a widely distributed native plant commonly found in moist, sandy soils of meadows, pastures, prairies, ditch and river banks and waste areas. The common licorice used to flavor candy is a different species, though the root of wild licorice is equally sweet and was an important food source for Native Americans.

Non-standard name: American licorice.

Alternate leaves are pinnately compound with 11 to 19 lanceolate leaflets.

Burs less than 3/4 inch long appear in August and September on wild licorice.

Hogpotato
Hoffmanseggia glauca (Ortega) Eifert

Hogpotato
Fabaceae
(Pea family)

A low-growing weak-stemmed perennial up to 1 foot tall, that reproduces from seed or underground tubers. The plant has bipinnately compound subbasal leaves, 5 to 10 inches long, arranged as odd-bipinnate or pinnae with 2 to 6 pairs plus 1; leaflets 6 to 11 pairs. Leaflets are oblong from 1/8 to 1/4 inch long and with glandular dots. Flowers are pea-like, yellow or red-orange, about 1/2 inch long. Pods are about 1 1/2 inches long containing dark reddish-brown seeds. Seeds are smooth, and egg-shaped, up to 1/8 inch long.

Hogpotato is a native weed of the Southwest and is found in large colonies growing in alkaline soil along roadsides and ditchbanks.

Synonym: *Hoffmanseggia densiflora.* Benth. ex Gray.

Seedling plants have bipinnately compound leaves with small pairaed leaflets.

Hogpotato has pea-like yellow to orange flowers.

331

Everlasting peavine
Lathyrus latifolius L.

Everlasting peavine
Fabaceae
(Pea family)

A perennial with stems 2 to 7 feet long that are broadly winged, with a more or less climbing growth habit. The 2 leaflets are broadly lance-shaped with stipules 1 to 2 inches long. Tendrils are well developed. Flowers (5 to 15 per cluster) are approximately 1 inch long, white, pink or red.

This native of Europe is our common weedy member of this genus.

Non-standard name: perennial peavine.

Sweetpea-like flowers of everlasting peavine vary from white to red.

Well developed tendrils and lance-shaped leaves are useful in the identification of the plant.

333

Wyeth lupine
Lupinus wyethii S. Wats.

Wyeth lupine
Fabaceae
(Pea family)

A perennial plant reproducing by seeds. Stems are upright and branched, often forming large showy clumps up to 18 inches in height. Flowers range from white to purple on Wyeth lupine which are more open than those of other species. Leaflets and stems are covered with fine hair. Palmate leaves are composed of 6 to 8 leaflets radiating from a central point. Flowers mature from the bottom of the plant to the top forming hairy pods containing several round seeds.

Silver lupine (*L. argenteus* Pursh) is another species very common in the West. Hungry sheep are often poisoned by lupine plants when being trailed through ranges in late summer. Cows eating lupines during early pregnancy sometimes have calves with skeletal defects. Lupines contain poisonous alkaloids throughout the growing season and even though there are some species that are not poisonous, precautions should always be taken with livestock. Poisoning can occur in sheep ingesting less than 1/4 pound of the plants, while cattle must eat over 1 pound for poisoning to occur. Control of lupine with herbicides should be done before the bud stage of growth.

Generally lupines have palmate leaves composed of 6 or 8 leaflets radiating from a central point.

Flower color varies from white to blue and white on Wyeth lupine as well as other species of lupine.

335

Black medic
Medicago lupulina L.

Black medic
Fabaceae
(Pea family)

A low trailing annual or short-lived perennial reproducing from seeds. Stems prostrate, 4-angled, branching from the base and radiating out from a taproot, 1 to 2 feet in length. Leaves are compound with 3 oval-shaped leaflets which are finely toothed and have prominent veins. The central leaflet is borne on a short stalk. Flowers are small and bright yellow, about 1/8 inch long, borne in clusters about 1/2 to 3/4 inch long. Flowers produce small pods which are kidney-shaped, thick-walled and curved. The pods are hairy but not spined and contain one seed.

The spiny pods of California burclover (*M. hispida* Gaertn.) differentiate it from black medic. Black medic and California burclover are natives of eastern Europe and Asia. They are found in the western United States and are a nuisance in lawns and gardens and along roadsides and waste areas. Flowering occurs from April to September.

Yellow flowers of black medic are about 1/8 inch long and produce small kidney-shaped pods.

California burclover has spiny curved seedpods.

Yellow sweetclover
Melilotus officinalis (L.) Lam.

Yellow sweetclover
Fabaceae
(Pea family)

An annual, winter annual, or biennial legume normally growing 2 to 6 feet tall. Trifoliate leaves resemble those of alfalfa, except that leaflet margins are serrated halfway or more back from the tip. Flowers are small, yellow (often fading to cream color), and arranged in many-flowered terminal and axillary racemes. Pods are 1- or 2-seeded, and cross-ribbed.

White sweetclover (*M. alba* Medic.) is similar to yellow sweetclover, but has white flowers and net-veined pods. Indian sweetclover (*M. indica* (L.) All.) is a less common species with yellow flowers, and net-veined pods. The sweetclovers were introduced from Europe and Asia, becoming common along roadsides and waste areas. Sweetclover is often one of the first plants to appear on disturbed sites, and is sometimes promoted for soil stabilization or soil improvement. It is also favored by honey producers. The common sweetclovers, often causing bloat in cattle, are high in coumarin which causes anticoagulation of blood. Commercially improved forage varieties have been developed with reduced levels of coumarin and are less likely to cause bloat.

Flower color is used to identify white sweetclover (left) and yellow sweetclover (center). Following flowering seedpods develop (bottom).

Sweetclover leaf (right) with leaflet margins serrated more than halfway back from tip. Alfalfa leaf (left) with leaflet margins serrated less than halfway back from tip.

Silky crazyweed
Oxytropis sericea Nutt. ex T. & G.

Silky crazyweed and Lambert crazyweed
Fabaceae
(Pea family)

Silky crazyweed and Lambert crazyweed, *O. lambertii* Pursh, are perennial herbaceous legumes common on western rangelands. Mature plants range in height from 6 to 12 inches. Leaves are covered with fine hairs giving it a whitish-gray appearance. Flowers vary in color by species, with silky crazyweed having white flowers and Lambert crazyweed having purplish-pink flowers. Flowers are borne on a leafless stalk emerging from the center of the plant, forming a spike-like cluster. The plant produces kidney-shaped seeds which are formed in a hairy, leather-like pod.

All livestock species can be poisoned by eating crazyweed. Horses never recover once they are poisoned. Cattle gain weight slowly and often have abortions, while sheep abortions are common from eating these plants. Livestock generally avoid eating crazyweed until feed is scarce, but once they have eaten it, they seek out the plants. Herbicides should be applied to actively growing plants, but before they reach the bud stage.

Non-standard name: locoweed.

Early growth stage of silky crazyweed is shown. Pinnately compound leaflets are covered with fine hair.

Lambert crazyweed flowers are purplish-pink and appear in mid-summer.

341

Honey mesquite
Prosopis glandulosa Torr.

Honey mesquite
Fabaceae
(Pea family)

A spiny deciduous shrub or small tree up to 30 feet or more in height and having a trunk up to 4 feet in diameter. Branches are armed with 1 to 2 straight, yellowish, 1/4- to 3-inch spines at each node. Leaves alternate, petiolate, compound with 6 to 20 pairs of leaflets arranged on both sides of the stem axis, and each leaflet finely hairy or hairless and 1/8 to 3/4 inch long. Small greenish flowers, sessile or pedicellate, are crowded on stems 2 to 5 inches long. Oblong, flat, tan, leathery seedpods (legumes) are finely hairy or hairless and 3 to 8 inches long.

Infrequent to abundant on a variety of soils, honey mesquite is a native woody plant that is more commonly found on dry ranges in the Southwest. Mesquite pods are relished by all livestock. Unlike most other pea pods, they do not shed their seeds. Associated species include western honey mesquite (*P. glandulosa* var. *torreyana* (L. Benson) M.C. Johnston) and velvet mesquite (*P. velutina* Woot.). Mesquite is considered weedy on rangeland because of its ability to compete for soil moisture and its reproductive ability. It grows well on dry sites and resprouts if complete root kill is not achieved.

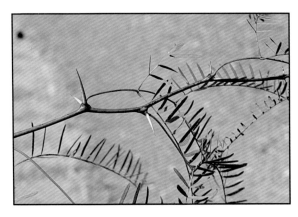

Yellowish spines up to 3 inches long are characteristically found on mature plants.

The beans of mesquite are edible and readily eaten by livestock. The digestive process scarifies the seed, allowing them to germinate the following year.

343

Swainsonpea
Sphaerophysa salsula (Pall.) DC.

Swainsonpea
Fabaceae
(Pea family)

Swainsonpea is a creeping perennial reproducing by seeds and lateral roots. Leaves are compound, composed of numerous opposite leaflets which are oval and covered with hair. Flowers occur from May to July, are 1/4 to 1 inch in length and are orange-red. Many seeds are formed in bladder-like translucent pods. Seeds are green with an attachment indentation.

This plant was introduced from Asia and is commonly found in some western states along roadsides and fences. It is a potential threat to alfalfa seed producing areas; the seed is a contaminant in alfalfa seed which is the same size, shape and weight, making it impossible to separate.

Green seeds nearly the same size as alfalfa seeds can be seen through translucent bladder-like pods in mid-summer.

Orange-red showy flowers, 1/4 to 1 inch long, appear from May to July.

Goldenpea
Thermopsis rhombifolia Nutt. ex Richards.

Goldenpea
Fabaceae
(Pea family)

Goldenpea is a rhizomatous perennial herb with 1 to 5 stems, erect from the crown, 6 to 16 inches tall. Leaves and stems are usually without hair. Leaves alternate and trifoliate, leaflets broadly elliptic, 1/2 to 1 inch long, 1/3 to 2/3 inch wide. Flowers in clusters up to 4 inches long, containing 10 to 30 individual yellow flowers.

A common native plant on roadsides, pastures and rangeland, ranging from Wyoming to New Mexico. It is not palatable to livestock and is sometimes competitive with more desirable vegetation. Flowering occurs from April to June. Mountain thermopsis (*T. montana* Nutt.) is similar to goldenpea, but has straight rather than curved pods and is poisonous to livestock.

Goldenpea leaves contain three leaflets. The plant may have up to 5 stems coming from the same crown.

Goldenpea is highly competitive and populations often cover large areas of range or pasture land.

Gorse

Ulex europaeus L.

Gorse
Fabaceae
(Pea family)

Gorse is a many-branched, rigid perennial often over 6 feet tall, with leaves modified into thorns. Flowers are bright yellow, pea-like, solitary or in clusters on short axillary stalks, developing into inch-long pods containing 1 to 4 seeds. When ripe, pods dehisce and eject seeds for some distance.

Gorse, native to Europe, was introduced into Hawaii as a hedge plant and into Oregon as an ornamental. It now infests many acres along the coasts of California, Oregon and Washington and upper elevation pasture lands on the islands of Hawaii and Maui, where it forms impenetrable stands due to its dense, thorny growth. Although goats and sheep will feed on its young growth, the plant is not grazed by other animals. Control of gorse is difficult due to its waxy cuticle (which inhibits herbicide penetration) and its production of large amounts of seed. Seeds are reported to stay viable in the soil for 30 years or more.

Gorse is impenetrable by animals because of its sharp thorns growing up to 3 inches long.

Yellow, pea-like flowers develop into 1 inch pods containing 1 to 4 seeds.

Hairy vetch
Vicia villosa Roth

Hairy vetch
Fabaceae
(Pea family)

A hairy annual with stems up to 6 feet long. Leaves have 10 to 20 leaflets which are linear to narrowly lance-shaped and 3/4 to 1 inch long. Tendrils are well developed. There are 20 to 60 flowers per cluster, all usually on one side of the stalk. Flowers are purplish-red and 3/4 to 1 inch long. Fruit is 3/4 to 1 inch long with several seeds.

Common vetch (*V. sativa* L.) is an escaped domestic species with larger seeds and leaves. Hairy vetch was brought from Europe to be used as a rotation crop. It has escaped and is now common along roadsides and on idle land. It persists because of its hard dormant seeds and is frequently a problem in cropland.

Non-standard names include: woolly vetch and winter vetch.

Flowers, leaves, and tendrils of hairy vetch are used in identifying this species.

The flowers and leaves of common vetch (shown here) are larger than those of hairy vetch.

Redstem filaree

Erodium cicutarium (L.) L'Her. ex Ait.

Redstem filaree
Geraniaceae
(Geranium family)

Winter annual or biennial with stems 1 inch to 2 feet long, spreading or erect, generally from a rosette. Leaves are divided into narrow feather-like lobed or toothed segments, both leaves and stems are hairy. Flowers are purplish-pink and generally borne in clusters of 2 or more. The fruit is 5-lobed and long-beaked, with each lobe splitting away at maturity.

A native of Europe or Asia, redstem filaree is common worldwide. It has been grown for forage and is considered noxious only when it crowds out more valuable crops.

Non-standard name: storksbill.

Flowers are generally borne in clusters of 2 or more.

The beaked fruit splits at maturity into five, one-seeded sections with coiled appendages.

Rocky Mountain iris
Iris missouriensis Nutt.

Rocky Mountain iris
Iridaceae
(Iris family)

A perennial from stout, branching rhizomes, stems 1 to 2 feet tall, nearly leafless. Basal leaves 1/4 to 1/2 inch wide. Flowers 1 to 4 per stem, blue-violet, 2 to 3 inches long.

Widespread in mountain meadows east of the Cascades, they are common along streambanks and in seepage areas on rangeland. In addition to being highly competitive with grasses they often cause problems when cutting hay. Rocky Mountain iris has been reported toxic to cattle.

Non-standard names: iris, wild iris.

Spreading of wild iris from branched rhizomes is common.

One to four flowers occur on each stem, blue-violet and 2 to 3 inches long.

355

Rush

Juncus spp.

Rush
Juncaceae
(Rush family)

Perennial or rarely annual low growing herbs with erect stems, perennials with rhizomatous roots. Leaves are located on basal portions of the plant and can be flat, folded, rolled or round. The seedheads appear near the top of stems, flowers are numerous as clusters subtended by several leafy or chaffy bracts.

There are over 300 species of *Juncus* world-wide. Most are found in moist sites but certain species grow on dry sites. Forage value is low, having limited use by livestock as hay and forage. Because rushes often grow in wet sites they are difficult to control with herbicides.

Non-standard name: wiregrass.

Leaves are found at the base of the plant. Stems are round in cross-section.

Mature fruit is surrounded by chaffy bracts.

357

Toad rush

Juncus bufonius L.

Toad rush
Juncaceae
(Rush family)

An annual 1 to 8 inches tall with branched stems. Leaf blades flat, less than 1/16 inch wide and up to 4 inches long. Flowers are usually borne singly and subtended by 2 bracts. The fruit is not angled, opening along 3 lines to release numerous minute seeds.

Found in wet soils throughout most of North America. It is especially common in lawns and gardens along coastal areas.

The fruit opens along 3 lines to release numerous minute seeds.

Mature plants are tufted with inconspicuous leaves and seedpods which are subtended by 2 bracts.

Seaside arrowgrass
Triglochin maritima L.

Seaside arrowgrass
Juncaginaceae
(Arrowgrass family)

Seaside arrowgrass is a native perennial, reproducing from rhizomes and seeds. Roots are short and fibrous. Basal leaves thick and succulent, having a round appearance but a rounded indentation on one side. Small, green, inconspicuous flowers are borne on stalks 1 to 3 feet high. Fruit borne in small pods having 6 compartments, each containing a single seed. The pods surround the seed stalk, but each is attached by a short pedicel or stalk.

Seaside arrowgrass grows in patches in wet alkaline soils, starting growth in early spring with flowering and seed formation occurring in late summer. The plant contains hydrocyanic acid, especially when drought- or frost-stressed, making it highly poisonous to livestock. As little as 1/4 pound of the stressed plants is capable of causing sudden death in yearling cattle if eaten in a short period of time. The poison, which causes respiratory failure, does not accumulate in the animal. Cured hay containing seaside arrowgrass has been reported toxic to young livestock. Two other species, arrowgrass (*T. concinna* Davy var. *debilis* (M.E. Jones) Howell) and marsh arrowgrass (*T. palustris* L.) are more delicate and slender than seaside arrowgrass.

Leaves of seaside arrowgrass resemble grass leaves, but they are fleshy with a semi-circular groove down each leaf.

Fruits are individually connected to a main stem by a pedicel or short stem.

Henbit
Lamium amplexicaule L.

Henbit
Lamiaceae
(Mint family)

An annual with spreading or weakly erect, 4-angled stems, much-branched at the base. Leaves opposite, the lower ones long petioled, more or less rounded in outline, coarsely toothed or lobed, upper leaves similar in outline, but sessile and clasping the stem. Flowers pink to purple and white, 2-lipped, 1/2 to 3/4 inch long, borne in compact whorls in the axils of the upper leaves. Each of the 4 brown and white mottled nutlets produced by each flower are narrow at the base.

Fields and waste places are common habitats of this species. Even though henbit was introduced from Eurasia and North Africa, it has become well established throughout North America. It is a problem weed of cropland, gardens, and in newly seeded lawns. It appears in early spring and flowers from April to July.

Leaves are coarsely toothed and clasp the square stem.

Flowers are pink to purple and white, 2-lipped from 1/2 to 3/4 inch long and are in compact whorls in the axils of upper leaves.

363

Purple deadnettle
Lamium purpureum L.

Purple deadnettle
Lamiaceae
(Mint family)

An annual with square stems, usually branched from the base. Leaves are opposite and mostly crowded near the top, with lower leaf petioles longer than upper ones. Upper leaves are usually purplish. Flowers are 2-lipped, mostly 3/8 to 5/8 inch long, pink to purple and borne in the axils of upper leaves. The fruit consists of 4 nutlets.

Purple deadnettle is native to Europe and is established in North America. It often forms a showy ground cover in early spring in gardens, orchards, and fields. Henbit (*L. amplexicaule* L.) is similar to purple deadnettle but can be distinguished by upper leaves having no petioles.

Non-standard name: red deadnettle.

The square stem and opposite leaves of purple deadnettle are good identification characteristics.

A typical patch of purple deadnettle in early spring appears light purple.

White horehound

Marrubium vulgare L.

White horehound
Lamiaceae
(Mint family)

An erect perennial 1 to 2 1/2 feet tall. Stems are 4-sided, woolly, and have a somewhat woody base. Leaves have petioles and are paired at each stem joint. Leaves have a white-woolly wrinkled surface and coarsely-toothed margins. Flowers are small, white, and borne in dense clusters in the leaf axils. The calyx of each flower surrounds the fruit and develops a whorl of small hooked spines, forming a characteristic cluster of bur-like structures in each leaf axil.

White horehound is a native of Europe that was probably introduced into the United States as a garden herb. It escaped cultivation and has become widely distributed along roadsides, dry waste areas, and in gardens.

Flowers and bur-like fruits develop as clusters in leaf axils.

The white-woolly stems are square when viewed in cross section.

Mediterranean sage
Salvia aethiopis L.

Mediterranean sage
Lamiaceae
(Mint family)

An aromatic biennial, growing 2 to 3 feet tall. In the first season it develops a rosette of large grayish woolly leaves. In the second season the plant bolts, producing multi-branched stems with white to blue-green, woolly, felt-like leaves. Lower leaves have petioles, are lobed with coarsely-toothed blades 1/3 to 1 foot long. Upper leaves are smaller and clasp the stem. The upper surface of leaves may eventually shed some of the pubescence, revealing the green wrinkled leaf. Flowers are yellowish-white, borne in clusters on profusely branched stems. The 4 nutlets, developing from each flower, are smooth with dark veins. One plant may produce thousands of seeds which are spread easily because the mature plant forms a tumbleweed.

Mediterranean sage is a native of the Mediterranean or northern Africa. It is spreading rapidly in many parts of the West, invading pastures, meadows, rangeland, and other open areas. Meadow sage (*S. pratensis* L.) resembles Mediterranean sage, but usually has blue flowers, and is more coarsely hairy.

Non-standard name: African sage.

Hooded "2-lipped" flowers are white to yellowish-white.

Rosettes have woolly, blue-green, felt-like leaves.

Lanceleaf sage
Salvia reflexa Hornem.

Lanceleaf sage
Lamiaceae
(Mint family)

Lanceleaf sage is a native annual, reproducing from seed. The stem is 4-sided and greatly branched. Leaves are opposite, lance-shaped with a blunt tip and narrow at the base, are 1 to 2 inches long and are both toothed and entire. Flowers are bell-shaped, 1/3 to 1/2 inch long, with an extended lower lip. They are usually opposite but sometimes have up to 4 flowers together, arranged in a whorl. When mature, each fruit is made up of 4 nutlets surrounded by dry chaffy bracts.

Sometimes called blue sage, it is common throughout the Rocky Mountain region, growing at elevations from 3,500 to 8,000 feet. The plant has a strong aroma and is normally unused by livestock. Livestock have been poisoned when lanceleaf sage is chopped or mixed with other feed. It is reported to contain large amounts of nitrates. Symptoms include muscular weakness followed by sudden death.

Seedlings have a 4-sided stem with opposite lance-shaped leaves with a blunt tip which narrows at the base.

Flowers are bell-shaped, on short stalks, ranging from 1/3 to 1/2 inch long. When mature, each fruit is made up of 4 nutlets surrounded by dry chaffy bracts.

Prairie onion
Allium textile Nels. & Macbr.

Prairie onion
Liliaceae
(Lily family)

Prairie onion is a native perennial reproducing by bulbs, aerial bulblets, and seed. The underground single bulb has no bulblets which are common on wild garlic. Leaves are fleshy and the whole plant has a strong onion odor. White flowers are borne on leafless flower stalks up to 18 inches tall. Seeds are black, 1/8 inch long or longer, with sharp angles.

Prairie onion is common in meadows and pastures and sometimes found in grain fields. The plant causes a strong onion flavor in milk and is difficult to control. Several *Allium* species are common with flowers ranging in color from white to rose.

Underground bulbs are single, with no offsets.

White flower clusters, borne on leafless flower stalks, are surrounded by a thin membrane.

Wild garlic
Allium vineale L.

Wild garlic
Liliaceae
(Lily family)

Perennial from bulbs, often clustered together. The outer coat of a bulb is papery and brittle; individual bulblets are asymmetrical. Leaves are few, originating from the base of the stem and are long-pointed. The stem is slender and solid, up to 3 feet tall, bearing a terminal cluster of flowers. The flowers, all or in part, are replaced by small bulbils. The bulbils are shed to form new plants or sometimes sprout in the head to form a bushy mass of green seedlings. All parts of the plant have a strong odor.

Wild garlic was introduced from Europe by early settlers as a food flavoring. A problem of pastures and cultivated crops in the eastern U.S., Washington, Oregon, northern California, and a small area of Wyoming.

Flowers, all or in part, are replaced by aerial bulbils.

Large bulb and secondary bulbs from base of the plant; secondary bulbs are not found in prairie onion.

375

California false-hellebore
Veratrum californicum Durand

California false-hellebore
Liliaceae
(Lily family)

A stout, coarse perennial from short, thick rootstocks, with leafy stems 3 to 7 feet tall. Leaves 6 to 12 inches long and 1/2 to 2/3 as broad, strongly sheathing at the base. Inflorescence a dense branching panicle, 1 to 2 feet long, or in *Veratrum californicum* var. *caudatum* (Heller) C.L. Hitchc., the upper 1/3 to 1/2 a densely flowered raceme. Flowers 6-parted, white, yellowish or even greenish-tinged. Fruits 3/4 to 1 1/4 inches long, containing yellowish, winged seeds.

This native plant is found most commonly in swamps, creek bottoms, meadows and moist woodlands at medium altitudes in our mountainous areas. Falsehellebore is toxic to humans and livestock, the poison reaction occurring within 2 to 3 hours after the plant is consumed. It causes a congenital deformity in lambs known as "monkey face," as well as abortion, when pregnant ewes feed on the plant. Since it is commonly found in mountain meadows around watering places, it is readily accessible to grazing livestock. Flowering occurs from June to August.

Leaves are 6 to 12 inches long and 3 to 6 inches wide, with strong sheaths surrounding stems.

Flowers are 6-parted, white, yellowish to green-tinged at the top of the central stem.

Meadow deathcamas

Zigadenus venenosus S. Wats

Foothill deathcamas and meadow deathcamas
Liliaceae
(Lily family)

Foothill deathcamas, *Z. paniculatus*, and meadow deathcamas, native perennials, have underground scaly bulbs and emerge in early spring. Plants have 5 or 6 basal, thickened, V-creased leaves with a grass-like appearance. Plants reach heights of 2 feet. White to yellowish flowers are borne as a terminal cluster in early summer. Meadow deathcamas flowers have a panicle-like appearance with lower florets spaced apart from the terminal cluster while foothill deathcamas flowers form a terminal compact plume. The rough brown seeds are formed in a capsule.

All parts of the plant contain a poisonous alkaloid at all growth stages. Bulbs, often mistaken for wild onions, can cause severe illness in humans. Death-camas is often eaten by sheep or cattle in early spring before other plants start producing forage. Sheep are the most commonly poisoned, but cattle deaths have also been reported. Respiratory problems occur in sheep after eating 1/2 to 2 pounds of *Zigadenus* plants. Pastures containing death-camas should be sprayed in early spring and should not be grazed by sheep until late spring when more forage becomes available.

Leaves of immature plants have 5 or 6 V-creased leaves with a grass-like appearance.

Foothill deathcamas has a compact flower arrangement forming a single cluster rather than individual flowers up and down the terminal stem.

Purple loosestrife
Lythrum salicaria L.

Purple loosestrife
Lythraceae
(Loosestrife family)

A rhizomatous perennial with erect stems, often growing 6 to 8 feet tall, usually associated with moist or marshy sites. Leaves are simple, entire, and opposite or whorled. Rose-purple flowers having 5 to 7 petals are arranged in long vertical racemes.

Purple loosestrife, is an introduced European ornamental species that often escapes to aquatic sites such as streambanks or shorelines of shallow ponds. Infestations can become dense and impede water flow in canals and ditches. Reports of reduced habitat for wildlife use are common.

Non-standard name: purple lythrum.

Showy rose-purple flowers bloom in long vertical racemes.

Lance-shaped leaves have smooth margins.

Velvetleaf
Abutilon theophrasti Medicus

Velvetleaf
Malvaceae
(Mallow family)

This is an annual, completely covered with soft hairs, with stems erect, branched, 2 to 7 feet tall. Leaves alternate, heart-shaped, pointed at the apex, 5 inches or more in width and attached on slender petioles. Flowers are solitary in leaf axils with 5 yellow-orange petals and numerous fused stamens that form a tube. Fruit are rounded with 9 to 15 segments arranged in a disk, each containing 3 to 9 egg-shaped, somewhat flattened, rough gray-brown seeds.

Introduced into this country from Asia, velvetleaf is widely distributed in the central U.S., but is found only sparingly in the western U.S. Velvetleaf thrives on rich soils and is found in cultivated fields, gardens, fence rows and waste areas. The seeds retain their viability in soil for more than 50 years, making eradication difficult. Flowering and seed production occur from late June to October.

Velvet leaf seedlings are covered with soft hair, stems often have a purple tinge.

Yellow-orange flowers containing 5 petals appear in leaf axils from June to October.

383

Spurred anoda
Anoda cristata (L.) Schlecht.

Spurred anoda
Malvaceae
(Mallow family)

An erect annual, branching at the base, usually 1/4 to 3 1/2 feet tall. Leaves are alternate, 1 1/2 to 3 inches long, usually triangular in shape, with some arrowhead-shaped, others lance-shaped. Flowers are solitary on stalks, arising from the leaf axil and are purplish-red to bluish-violet. The 5 green outer flower parts are apparent, with the lobes widely spreading under and extending beyond the flattened disk of the fruit. The disks contain 8 to 20 carpels united in a ring, each conspicuously beaked with an elongated dorsal spur. Fruits break apart at maturity.

This plant, native of the Southwest, has spread from Iowa to Arizona. It is troublesome in crops, gardens, ditches, along roadsides and waste areas.

The leaves are triangular in appearance, though some may look more arrowhead- or lance-shaped.

The individual fruit structures (carpels) have a characteristic spur.

Venice mallow
Hibiscus trionum L.

Venice mallow
Malvaceae
(Mallow family)

An annual, typically growing 10 to 18 inches tall. Stems and petioles are usually covered with stiff hairs. Stems generally originate from a central base, and tend to be more spreading than erect. Leaves are deeply cleft into 3 or 5 coarsely toothed lobes. The showy flowers are light sulfur-yellow with a purple or blackish center, reaching up to 1 1/2 inches in diameter. Petals are shed soon after flowers open. Dark brown seeds develop within a large papery sac-like structure formed from the inflated calyx.

Venice mallow was introduced from Europe. It is typically found in waste areas, gardens, orchards, and cultivated fields.

Non-standard names: bladder ketmia, flower-of-an-hour, rosemallow.

Flowers are light sulfur-yellow with a deep purple center and golden anthers. Seeds develop in a strongly-veined, papery, inflated calyx.

Seedling plants have deeply lobed leaves.

Common mallow
Malva neglecta Wallr.

Common mallow
Malvaceae
(Mallow family)

Annual, winter annual biennial or perennial with stems generally low spreading, the branches erect from 2 to 20 inches long. Leaves long-petioled, rounded with a heart-shaped base, 3/4 to 3 1/2 inches in diameter, inconspicuously 5 to 7 lobed. Flower petals, ranging from white to pale lavender, are fused and about twice the length of the calyx. Fruit consists of a circle of rounded one-seeded lobes separating at maturity.

This species, introduced from Europe, has long been present in the U.S. It is common in waste areas, gardens and cultivated land.

A similar species, little mallow (*M. parviflora* L.), is less common and differs from common mallow by having shorter petals and the lobes of the fruit being flattened and wrinkled.

Non-standard names: buttonweed, cheeseplant.

Seedling plants, germinating in early spring, have round, lobed leaves with a V-notched base.

Lavender-striped flowers and round button-like fruit are formed in mid-summer.

389

Alkali sida
Sida hederacea (Dougl.) Torr.

Alkali sida
Malvaceae
(Mallow family)

A low-growing perennial, somewhat resembling common mallow. Foliage is densely hairy with prominent star-shaped hairs, giving leaves a gray-green color or sometimes the foliage may have a yellowish cast due to an abundance of scurfy yellow scales. Leaves have petioles, are fan-shaped or kidney-shaped, with toothed margins. Flowers are axillary. Petals are less than 1/2 inch long, whitish, yellow, or cream-colored; often fading or drying to pink.

Alkali sida is a native species that can become troublesome in meadows, pastures, and cultivated crops, especially in somewhat alkaline or saline soils.

Synonym: *Malva hederacea* Dougl., *Malvella leprosa* (Ortega) Krapov.

Non-standard name: dollar weed, alkali mallow.

Cream-colored flowers are 1/2 to 3/4 inch wide, with a ball-like cluster of stamens in the center.

Petioled leaves are fan-shaped with toothed margins. A dense covering of star-shaped hairs gives foliage a gray-green appearance.

Scarlet globemallow
Sphaeralcea coccinea (Nutt.) Rydb.

Scarlet globemallow
Malvaceae
(Mallow family)

These species are perennial herbs or woody but low, diminutively shrubby plants that are usually closely pubescent with star-shaped hairs. Leaves thick, shallowly toothed to palm-shaped with lateral lobes 2-cleft. Flower consists of a 5-lobed calyx with 5 petals, usually red (grenadine), sometimes pink or lavender. Carpels, 5 to 15, united in a ring around a central axis, often remaining attached to the axis after maturity by a thread-like extension of the dorsal nerve, are differentiated into 2 parts, the upper part seedless, smooth and dehiscent, while the lower part contains seed and is indehiscent.

These native species are difficult to distinguish due to the leaf variation that exists among them, with some of the more common species being scarlet globemallow (*S. coccinea* (Nutt.) Rydb.), narrowleaf globemallow (*S. angustifolia* (Cav.) G. Don), and Emory globemallow (*S. emoryi* Torr.). These species are common along roadsides and in rangeland but are not strongly competitive.

Variation among leaves makes identification difficult unless mature fruit is present.

Five-petal showy flowers are usually pomegranate red.

Fireweed
Epilobium angustifolium L.

Fireweed
Onagraceae
(Evening primrose family)

Perennial from spreading rootstocks with stems that are usually simple, up to 9 feet tall. Leaves are lance-shaped, entire or remotely toothed and up to 8 inches long. Flowers are showy, rose to purple and borne in a long terminal raceme, or with some flowers in the axils of the upper leaves. The fruit is 2 to 3 inches long, splitting open at maturity to release the numerous brown seeds, each with a tuft of fine, off-white hairs, aiding in their dispersal.

Common throughout the U.S., fireweed occurs on burned timberland, along roadsides and on wasteland. It is used by bees and is reported to be good sheep forage.

Non-standard name: blooming sally.

Terminal raceme of fireweed showing flowers and immature fruit.

The mature fruit splits to release numerous seeds, each bearing a tuft of hairs, aiding in their dispersal.

Velvety gaura
Gaura parviflora Dougl. ex Lehm.

Velvety gaura
Onagraceae
(Evening primrose family)

An erect biennial or winter annual that grows 5 to 6 feet high. Leaves are lance-shaped, with little or no petiole. Leaves and stems are covered with long, spreading, soft hairs. Flowers are small and numerous, borne on long spike-like inflorescences. Sepals and petals are both reddish, about 1/10 inch long. Flowers have 4 petals and 8 stamens. Seeds are retained in 4-angled, nut-like fruits.

Scarlet gaura (*G. coccinea* Nutt. ex Pursh) resembles small-flowered gaura, but branches more from the base, lacks spreading hairs on the stem, and has larger flowers. Small-flowered gaura is found in pastures, waste areas, along roadsides, and even in dryland wheat fields. Both species of *Gaura* are native to the United States.

Non-standard name: willow gaura, small-flowered gaura.

Numerous small 4-petalled flowers are borne on long spike-like inflorescences.

Leaves and stems are covered with long, soft, spreading hairs.

Creeping woodsorrel
Oxalis corniculata L.

Creeping woodsorrel
Oxalidaceae
(Woodsorrel family)

A prostrate creeping perennial from a slender taproot. Stems root at the joints. Leaves alternate and trifoliate with broad, heart-shaped leaflets borne at the tip of a long petiole. Leaves are green to purplish, often closing and drooping at night. Flowers have 5 yellow petals 1/8 to 1/3 inch long and occur in clusters of 1 to 5 at the ends of slender flower stalks. Seed pods are erect, hairy, cylindrical, 1/3 to 1 inch long, and pointed at the tip. When seeds are mature, pods open explosively, often spreading seeds more than 10 feet. Seeds are rough and reddish.

Yellow woodsorrel (*O. stricta* L.) resembles creeping woodsorrel but lacks stipules and normally does not root at the nodes. Creeping woodsorrel is a native of Europe and is distributed in the southwestern United States. Its habitats include lawns, flower beds, gardens and greenhouses.

Yellow 5-petalled flower and cylindrical seedpods of creeping woodsorrel.

Creeping woodsorrel often roots at the nodes.

399

Annual pricklepoppy
Argemone polyanthemos (Fedde) G.B. Ownbey

Annual pricklepoppy
Papaveraceae
(Poppy family)

Annual pricklepoppy has erect, prickly, sparingly branched stems up to 3 feet tall. The entire plant contains a yellow sap. Leaves are grayish-green, coarsely lobed, spiny on margins and midrib. Flowers are terminal, large, white. Seeds are small, round blackish-brown, ridged on one side.

Annual pricklepoppy is a native plant to the Rocky Mountain region, occurring in pastures, waste areas, and along roadsides. It is seldom abundant and can be an indicator of overgrazing. Its spines make it undesirable for livestock feed. The prickles have been known to irritate the skin of some people. Although it produces beautiful flowers, it is generally considered a nuisance because of its unpalatability.

Yellow spines along the main stem and leaves prevent livestock from using this plant.

Large showy flowers with many stamen blossom in late summer.

Buckhorn plantain
Plantago lanceolata L.

Buckhorn plantain
Plantaginaceae
(Plantain family)

This is a perennial from a stout fibrous rootstock. The crown of the plant is covered with tan woolly hairs. Leaves all basal, 3- to several-veined, narrowly elliptic or lance-elliptic, 4 to 12 inches long, usually less than 1 1/2 inches wide. Flowering stalks are several, up to 18 inches tall, bearing a dense spike of small flowers, subtended by thin ovate bracts; stamens, 4, exerted, conspicuous. Seeds, shiny, 4 per fruit, blackish, about 1/16 inch long.

Buckhorn plantain is native to Eurasia and is a weed of roadsides, pastures and other disturbed sites such as lawns and gardens. Flowering period is May to August.

Non-standard names: English plantain, lanceleaf plantain.

Seedlings of buckhorn plantain have long narrow leaves with prominent parallel veins.

Flowering begins in late summer. This ring of white flowers appears first at the base of the inflorescence but progresses to the tip.

403

Broadleaf plantain
Plantago major L.

Broadleaf plantain
Plantaginaceae
(Plantain family)

This is a fibrous-rooted perennial, from an erect caudex, the crown not woolly, sometimes blooming the first year. Leaves are all basal, broadly elliptic to ovate, blade abruptly contracted to the well-defined petiole. The blade is entire or irregularly toothed, 3 to 7 inches long, 3- to several-veined. The flowering stem is 5 to 15 inches long, topped with a dense, elongated spike of small flowers. Corolla lobes are papery, reflexed; stamens, 4, exerted. Fruit is 1/4 inch long; seeds 6 to 30, black or brown, strongly reticulate.

Broadleaf plantain is supposedly a native of Europe; but today it is cosmopolitan in distribution, inhabiting roadsides, lawns, disturbed sites and cultivated fields. It can be found in valleys to midmontane sites and flowers from April to September.

In early spring, this perennial forms a rosette which has leaves from 3 to 7 inches long with wavy margins and prominent veins.

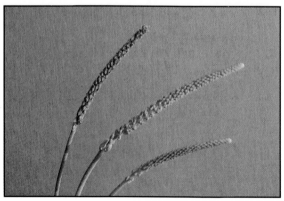

Inconspicuous flowers are borne on spike-like inflorescences.

Woolly plantain
Plantago patagonica Jacq.

Woolly plantain
Plantaginaceae
(Plantain family)

An annual, 3 to 10 inches tall, and covered with hairs. Leaves, 1 to 5 inches long, upright, narrow, pubescent and clustered at the base of the plant. Flowers are whitish, in spikes 1 to 5 inches long, and surrounded by woolly bracts.

Woolly plantain is a common invader of abused, native ranges. After maturity it is not utilized by livestock if other forage is available. This native warm-season forb is not a highly competitive species with native rangeland perennials. It grows on plains, slopes and is common on sandy soils. Flowers appear from May to July.

Leaves appear in late winter, are 1 to 5 inches long and narrow, and are clustered at the base of the plant.

Woolly bracts surround seedpods which contain two small seeds in each pod.

Jointed goatgrass

Aegilops cylindrica Host

Jointed goatgrass
Poaceae
(Grass family)

Jointed goatgrass is a winter annual, 15 to 30 inches tall with one to many erect stems or tillers. Leaves are alternate, simple, with auricles at the base and a leaf blade 1/8 to 1/4 inch wide, with hairs. The spike is cylindrical, more than 10 times as long as it is wide. It contains 2 to 12 spikelets that fit into the contour of the rachis, spikelets 1/2 inch long with 1 to 3 viable seeds. Glumes several-ribbed with a keel on one side extending into a single awn or beard. At maturity spikelets separate with a segment of the rachis still attached.

Jointed goatgrass is native to southern Europe, but it is now established in most winter wheat growing areas of North America, spread as a seed contaminant or by custom combiners. It is found mostly in wheat fields, but it survives along roadsides, in waste areas, alfalfa fields and pastures. The plant is most difficult to control in areas where winter wheat is grown continuously. Flowering and seed production may occur from May to July.

Non-standard name: jointgrass.

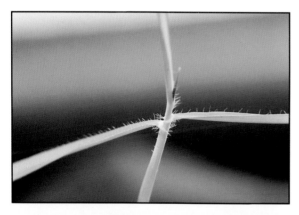

Immature jointed goatgrass plants have marginal hairs on the leaf and at the stem juncture.

Segmented, slender jointed goatgrass (left) compared to wheat at harvest time.

Quackgrass
Elytrigia repens (L.) Nevski

Quackgrass
Poaceae
(Grass family)

Quackgrass is an aggressive perennial grass reproducing by seed, or spreading by a shallow mass of long, slender, branching rhizomes. Rhizomes are usually yellowish-white, sharp-pointed, somewhat fleshy. They are able to penetrate hard soils or even tubers and roots of other plants. Stems are erect and usually 1 to 3 feet tall. Leaf blades are 1/4 to 1/2 inch wide, flat, pointed and have small auricles (ear-like appendages) at the junction of blade and sheath. Leaf sheaths and the upper surface of leaf blades may be thinly covered with soft hairs. Spikelets are arranged in two long rows, borne flatwise to the stem. Florets are awnless, or with short straight awns.

Quackgrass was introduced from the Mediterranean area. It has spread over much of North America, adapting well to moist soils in cool temperate climates. Quackgrass reduces productivity in crops, rangeland and pasture. It is also a nuisance in lawns, ornamentals and home gardens and is believed to be allelopathic. Because of the ability of broken rhizome segments to grow and produce new plants, it is extremely difficult to control mechanically.

Synonym: *Agropyron repens* (L.) Beauv.

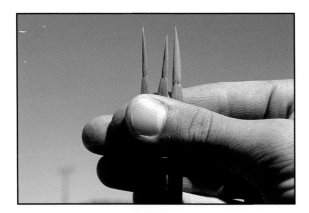

Quackgrass leaves are often constricted near the tips allowing for identification of vegetative stages.

New plants develop in dense stands from sharp-pointed, yellow-white rhizomes.

411

Creeping bentgrass
Agrostis stolonifera L.

Creeping bentgrass
Poaceae
(Grass family)

A low-growing perennial, 8 to 20 inches tall, from stolons which creep and root along the surface of the ground. The panicle is closed most of the season and open only when blooming. The leaf ligule is membranous, thin, 1/32 to 1/8 inch long, entire or finely toothed.

Colonial bentgrass (*A. tenuis* Sibth.) differs from creeping bentgrass in that it can spread by short rootstalks and rhizomes and has panicles that are open most of the season.

Non-standard name: seaside bentgrass.

Creeping bentgrass can be distinguished by its stoloniferous growth habit.

The panicles of colonial bentgrass are open most of the season compared to the closed panicles of creeping bentgrass.

413

Blackgrass

Alopecurus myosuroides Huds.

Blackgrass
Poaceae
(Grass family)

Annual with erect culms which are closely clustered, slightly rough to the touch and up to 2 feet tall. Leaf blades are usually 1/10 to 1/8 inch wide. The panicle is spikelike, somewhat tapering at each end and 1 to 4 inches long. The glumes are pointed, whitish with 3 green nerves; lemma is about as long as the glumes and the awn is bent.

Rare in the western U.S. but widespread and a serious problem in Europe.

Non-standard name: slender foxtail.

Panicle is slender, somewhat tapering at each end.

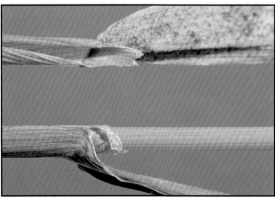

Smooth leaves have long papery ligules.

Tuber oatgrass
Arrhenatherum elatius (L.) Presl var. *bulbosum* (Willd.) Spenner

Tuber oatgrass
Poaceae
(Grass family)

Perennial with stems up to 6 feet tall, from bulbous bases, these bulb-like structures are often borne in short chains. Leaves with flat blades, roughened, 3/8 inch or less wide with short, membranous ligules. The panicle is 1/2 to 1 foot long and open, with short, whorled branches, these usually bear spikelets to the base; spikelets are 5/8 inch long with each spikelet having 2 florets, the lower floret with a bent awn.

Tuber oatgrass is a native of Europe that can be found throughout the Pacific Northwest. It occurs on roadsides, in waste areas and in cultivated fields. It is difficult to control because the bulbs are spread as the soil is tilled by farm equipment.

Bulb-like root structures in chains resembling strings of beads are found near the soil surface.

The inflorescence with whorled branches usually bears florets at the base of each branch.

Wild oat
Avena fatua L.

Wild oat
Poaceae
(Grass family)

Wild oat is an annual, 1 to 4 feet tall with erect hollow stems. Leaf blades are 1/8 to 5/8 inch wide, sheaths open, ligules membranous. The seedling leaves twist counterclockwise. The inflorescence is an open panicle, 4 to 18 inches long, drooping, spikelets contain 2 to 3 florets which disarticulate above the glumes. Seeds are yellow to black, narrowly oval, 1/4 to 1/2 inch long.

This species is distinguished from domestic oats by the twisted awn which bends at right angles and a horseshoe-shaped scar at its seed base. Slender oat (*A. barbata* Brot.) has smaller florets and a more slender rachis. Wild oat is a native of Europe, but is common throughout much of western North America. It is a serious problem in spring-seeded small grain, but it also occurs along roadsides, in pastures and waste areas. Seed can remain dormant in the soil for as long as 10 years, making it difficult to eliminate once established. Flowering and seed production occur from June to August.

Seedling leaves twist counterclockwise when viewed from above the plant stem.

Spikelets contain two or three seeds which have awns that form right angles at maturity.

419

California brome
Bromus carinatus H. & A.

California brome
Poaceae
(Grass family)

California brome is a perennial, 20 to 40 inches tall. Leaf blades are 8 to 12 inches long and 3/8 to 1/2 inch wide, rough or sparsely hairy. Inflorescence 6 to 12 inches long with spreading or drooping branches. Spikelets are 3/8 to 1 inch long, broad and flat with sharply keeled lemmas, awns 1/4 to 5/8 inch long.

This highly variable grass invades open waste areas and cropland. In the vegetative stage it is difficult to distinguish from several other weedy bromes. Seed germination usually occurs in the fall; young plants over-winter, grow rapidly in the spring and reach maturity by early summer. It is a vigorous competitor throughout the West and is palatable throughout its life cycle.

Non-standard name: mountain brome.

California brome spikelets are compressed with sharpened edges.

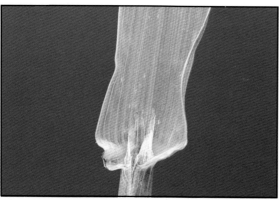

The ligule and tiny auricles shown are typical of California brome but are not positive identification for separating Bromus species.

Rescuegrass
Bromus catharticus Vahl

Rescuegrass
Poaceae
(Grass family)

Rescuegrass is an annual or short-lived perennial, up to 40 inches tall. Leaf blades are 8 to 12 inches long and 3/8 to 1/2 inch wide, rough or sparsely hairy. Inflorescence open and up to 8 inches long. Spikelets are 3/4 to 1 inch long, broad and flat with sharply keeled lemmas. Spikelets are awnless or with awns to 1/8 inch.

Rescuegrass was introduced from South America and is cultivated as a winter forage in the southern states; it is similar to California brome. Seeds germinate in the fall, young plants grow slowly throughout the winter and make rapid growth in the spring maturing in the early summer. If they are harvested or grazed, the plants will continue to be vegetative and produce forage into the fall.

The spikes are compressed and sharply keeled as with California brome.

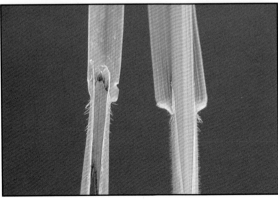

The ligule and tiny auricles are typical of rescuegrass, but are not positive characteristics for separating Bromus species.

423

Japanese brome
Bromus japonicus Thunb.

Japanese brome
Poaceae
(Grass family)

Japanese brome is an annual or winter annual, 14 to 30 inches tall. It reproduces by seed. Leaf blades and sheaths are soft and hairy. Inflorescence diffuse, 4 1/2 to 8 inches long with 3 to 5 lower, usually drooping branches. Spikelets are 1/4 inch wide and about 1/2 inch long, awns are 1/4 to 3/4 inch long, somewhat twisted and widely spreading at maturity.

This European introduction has become a nuisance in depleted ranges, hayfields, and dry soils in waste or disturbed areas. It is often confused with downy brome. Seed germination usually occurs in the fall; young plants overwinter, grow rapidly in the spring and reach maturity by June. It occurs throughout the West and is only palatable in the early stages of growth before seeds dry in the spring. A vigorous cover of desirable, perennial grasses is a good method of prevention in pastures and rangelands.

Stems and leaves are covered with soft hairs at all growth stages.

Mature spikelets about 1/2 inch long have awns from 1/4 to 3/4 inch long.

Soft brome
Bromus mollis L.

Soft brome
Poaceae
(Grass family)

An annual, up to 3 feet tall, softly pubescent throughout. Panicle erect with crowded spikelets 3/8 to 7/8 inch long. Glumes are distinctly broad and blunt. Awns are 1/4 to 1/2 inch long.

This European introduction is widespread in the region as a weed of waste land and cultivated fields. Seed germination usually occurs in the fall; young plants then overwinter, grow rapidly in the spring and reach maturity in early summer.

Non-standard names: soft cheat and soft chess.

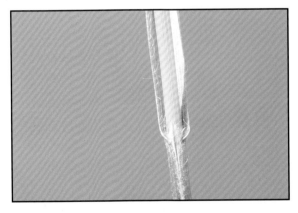

Leaf sheaths are closed with spreading hairs. The ligule is membranous up to 1 mm long.

Spikes are pubescent, rounded and uncompressed along the outer margin.

Ripgut brome
Bromus rigidus Roth

Ripgut brome
Poaceae
(Grass family)

Ripgut brome is an annual growing 1 to 3 feet tall. Leaf blades are flat, with sheaths that are usually hairy, 1/8 to 1/2 inch wide with soft, straight hairs. Ligules are membranous, unevenly fringed, 1/8 to 1/4 inch long. The inflorescence is open, with spreading, or drooping branches bearing 1 to 2 spikelets. Spikelets, 1 1/4 to 1 1/2 inches long, have 5 to 8 awned florets. Awns up to 2 1/4 inches are stout and rough-textured.

Ripgut brome is native to Europe and northern Africa. It is common along the Pacific coast of North America, occurring from British Columbia south to Mexico with isolated infestations found in other western states. Ripgut brome is a common weed of waste areas, roadsides and railroads, and is invasive on rangelands. The long stiff awns at maturity can cause injury to the nose and eyes of grazing animals.

Synonym: *Bromus diandrus* Roth.

Ligules are membranous and unevenly fringed while leaf blades and sheaths have soft, spreading hairs.

Individual spikelets have multiple florets, each having long offensive awns.

Cheat
Bromus secalinus L.

Cheat
Poaceae
(Grass family)

An annual up to 30 inches tall. Leaves are 1/8 to 1/4 inch wide and sparsely hairy. Panicle is nodding and open. Spikelets are 1/2 to 3/4 inch long and 1/4 to 3/8 inch wide. Margins of lemmas are deeply in-rolled at maturity in contrast to most bromes in our region. Awns are 1/8 to 1/4 inch long.

Although introduced from Europe it is common throughout most of the United States. Seeds usually germinate in the fall; young plants overwinter, grow rapidly in the spring, and reach maturity by early summer.

Non-standard name: chess.

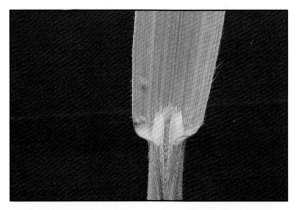

The ligule and tiny auricles are typical of many of the bromes.

The spikes of cheat are smooth with short awns.

Downny brome

Bromus tectorum L.

Downy brome
Poaceae
(Grass family)

Downy brome is an annual or winter annual, 4 to 30 inches tall, reproducing by seed. Leaf sheaths and flat blades are densely covered with soft hair. Ligules are short. Inflorescence is dense, slender, usually drooping, 1-sided, 2 to 6 inches long. Spikelets are nodding, slender 3/8 to 3/4 inch long. Awns are 3/8 to 5/8 inch long, usually purplish at maturity.

Downy brome was introduced from the Mediterranean region in packing material and first found near Denver, Colorado. It is now widely distributed throughout North America and is common along roadsides, waste areas, misused pastures and rangelands, and cultivated crop areas. Although downy brome is considered an invader, on certain intermountain ranges it has become the primary green forage utilized by livestock. The plant competes with more desirable perennial grasses for moisture because of its winter and early spring growth habit. After maturity it becomes a nuisance and a fire hazard. It is also a common crop seed contaminant very difficult to separate from grass seed.

Non-standard name: cheatgrass.

Plants are covered with soft hairs at all growth stages.

Mature downy brome seedheads, 2 to 6 inches long, contain seed, 3/8 to 3/4 inch long, with awns up to 5/8 inch long.

Longspine sandbur
Cenchrus longispinus (Hack.) Fern.

Longspine sandbur
Poaceae
(Grass family)

A warm-season annual grass with tufted stems. It grows 8 inches to 3 feet tall, occasionally erect, but usually spreading horizontally and forming dense mats. Leaf sheaths are flattened, very loose, smooth with hairy margins. Leaf blades are flat, roughened, 2 to 6 inches long and 1/4 inch wide with rounded margins. The spikes are 1 to 3 inches long and bear clusters of 10 to 30 burs. Burs are thickly set with stiff, sharp, spreading spines. They usually contain two light brown, oval to oblong seeds.

A native of Europe, longspine sandbur is a nuisance throughout most of the U.S. It grows in cultivated fields, pastures and waste areas; but favors sandy or well-drained, gravelly soils. It can be particularly troublesome to livestock causing injury to mouths, noses or eyes that come in contact with the mature burs. The presence of burs also reduces the value of wool. Sandbur is commonly spread by animals and machinery. Flowering and seed production occur from July to September.

Other sandbur species in the West include: field sandbur (*C. incertus* M.A. Curtis).

Immature plants, often purplish, have flattened stems usually spreading horizontally.

Longspine sandbur spikes are 1 to 3 inches long with 10 to 30 burs contained in each cluster.

435

Bermudagrass
Cynodon dactylon (L.) Pers.

Bermudagrass
Poaceae
(Grass family)

A wiry perennial with long, slender, creeping rhizomes and stolons. Leaves are generally smooth, with a conspicuous ring of white hairs at the junction of blade and sheath. Decumbent stems typically have papery leaf sheaths at each node. Decumbent stems spread laterally over the soil surface, rooting freely at lower nodes. Flowering stems are upright and bear a terminal group of 3 to 7 spike-like branches, usually originating in a single whorl on the ends of stems (in a configuration resembling fingers on a hand). Individual spikes are 1 to 2 inches long and bear 2 rows of sessile spikelets along one side of a somewhat flattened rachis.

Bermudagrass was probably introduced from Africa. It is widely established in warmer regions of the West and Southwest, where it is frequently used as a pasture or lawn grass. More recently it has become established in colder regions of the West, posing a serious threat to crop production and turf management. Bermudagrass is sometimes confused with large crabgrass (*Digitaria sanguinalis* (L.) Scop.) because of a superficial resemblance between inflorescences, and both have prostrate spreading stems that may root at nodes. Crabgrass spikelets are attached to the rachis by an obvious short pedicel.

Stolons spread laterally over the ground, rooting freely at any node.

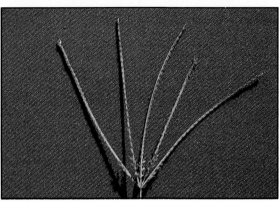

The flowering stems are upright and bear a terminal group of 4 or 5 spikes up to 2 inches long.

Orchardgrass
Dactylis glomerata L.

Orchardgrass
Poaceae
(Grass family)

Tufted perennial with stems up to 4 feet tall. Leaves are more or less roughened, sheaths flattened and keeled, and blades are 1/8 to 1/2 inch wide. Flowers are borne in 1-sided clusters on stiff panicle branches.

This Eurasian species is widely cultivated for pastures and as hay. It has, however, commonly escaped and is more or less weedy along roadsides and in disturbed habitats throughout most of the United States.

Non-standard name: cock's foot.

Spikelets are arranged as 1-sided clusters on stiff panicle branches.

Leaves of orchardgrass are flattened, keeled and folded.

439

Large crabgrass
Digitaria sanguinalis (L.) Scop.

Large crabgrass
Poaceae
(Grass family)

A summer annual, 6 inches to 2 feet in height, which reproduces by seeds. It often roots along the stem spreading from the plant base. Leaf blades are flat and 1/4 to 1/2 inch wide with sheaths that have long stiff hairs. The inflorescence is made up of 3 to 11 slender finger-like spikes or branches, 2 to 6 inches long, most arising from the same point at the stem tip but may have several additional branches below the stem tip. The small spikelets are 1/8 to 3/16 inch long and lie along only one side of the spike or flowering branch. The seed is oval and about 1/12 inch long.

Smooth crabgrass (*D. ischaemum* (Schreb. ex Schweig.) Schreb. ex Muhl. is similar to large crabgrass but the leaves are smaller and not hairy. Large crabgrass was introduced from Europe and is a weed in lawns and cultivated fields in the western United States.

Inflorescence of large crabgrass with slender finger-like spikes, some of which arise slightly below the stem tip.

Leaves of large crabgrass (left) are hairy and larger than those of smooth crabgrass (right).

Saltgrass
Distichlis spicata (L.) Greene

Saltgrass
Poaceae
(Grass family)

A low, stiff perennial 4 to 16 inches high, reproducing by seed and creeping underground rhizomes that root at the joints to produce new stems, often forming a dense colony. Leaves are alternate but come up the stem in 2 rows. They are 1/2 to 4 inches long and 1/8 inch wide, sometimes folded lengthwise or rolled inward. At the base of the leaf blade the collar or ligule forms a ring of white, twisted hairs. Saltgrass is one of a few species of grass that have separate male and female plants. The flower groups are similar in appearance. Spikelets are clustered at the top of the stems, are somewhat flattened, 1/3 to 1/4 inch long with 5 to 9 flowers per spikelet.

Saltgrass is found growing on saline and alkaline soils in the western United States and is common in alkaline soil or sometimes soils in drainage, flood plains, and marshes in the desert. As a weed it has spread to irrigated lands and is common in ditches and on the margins of cultivated fields.

Flower spikelets are clustered at the top of the stems.

Leaves are alternate but come up the stem in 2 rows. Saltgrass often spreads by creeping rhizomes.

Junglerice
Echinochloa colona (L.) Link

Junglerice
Poaceae
(Grass family)

A summer annual 2 to 3 feet tall. Leaf blades are smooth and flat, about 1/4 inch wide and 3 to 6 inches long. Leaves often contain purple bands or stripes that are perpendicular to the length of the leaf. Leaf sheaths are lacking auricles or ligules. The panicle is 2 to 6 inches long with short branches up to 1 inch long. The spikelets, which are about 1/8 inch in length, are crowded on the rachis in 2 to 4 regular rows.

The spikelets do not end in a bristle as does barnyardgrass, but they are sharp-pointed. Jungle rice is a native of Europe and can be found in cultivated fields and waste areas throughout the southwestern United States. Junglerice is called *E. colonum* in many publications but recent literature refers to it as *E. colona*.

Non-standard name: watergrass.

Small flat seedlings have purple striped leaves.

Short branched panicle having spikelets crowded along the rachis.

Barnyardgrass
Echinochloa crus-galli (L.) Beauv.

Barnyardgrass
Poaceae
(Grass family)

Barnyardgrass is a vigorous, warm season annual grass reaching 1 to 5 feet in height with bases of many stems reddish to dark purple. Leaf blades are flat, 3/8 to 5/8 inch broad, smooth, and without a ligule or auricles at the junction of sheath and blade. Leaf sheaths are open lacking auricles and ligules. Panicles are often reddish to dark purple. Spikelets are crowded; awns might be absent or can be found up to 1 inch long, stiff scattered hairs are common.

Barnyardgrass was introduced from Europe and has become widespread throughout our region, especially in irrigated crops, gardens and other cultivated areas.

Non-standard name: Japanese millet.

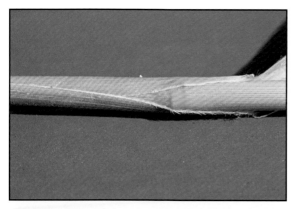

Leaf sheaths are open lacking auricles and ligules.

Seedheads, often purple, contain crowded large seeds.

Goosegrass
Eleusine indica (L.) Gaertn.

Goosegrass
Poaceae
(Grass family)

Spreading annual with flattened stems 15 to 36 inches long. Leaf blades are flat or folded, 1 to 3 inches long and 1/8 to 1/2 inch wide. Stems at maturity terminate in an inflorescence consisting of 2 to several stout spikes which are finger-like, sometimes with 1 or 2 spikes a short distance below the summit. Spikelets are compressed and form 2 rows along one side of the spike rachis.

Goosegrass is a native of the old world and common in lawns in the warmer parts of the western United States.

Non-standard name: silver crabgrass.

Spikelets are arranged in opposite rows along the axis of each spike. There are 2 to several spikes per inflorescence.

Leaves are generally smooth with a few long hairs on the leaf sheaths and a marginal fringe of shorter hairs.

Stinkgrass
Eragrostis cilianensis (All.) E. Mosher

Stinkgrass
Poaceae
(Grass family)

An annual with small glandular structures on the foliage and spikelets which give off a disagreeable odor. Stems hollow, 6 inches to 2 feet tall. Leaves flat to folded, 1/16 to 5/16 inch wide. Sheaths open, the ligule a fringe of straight hairs. Panicles congested, rounded to oblong, 1 1/2 to 9 inches long. Seed shatters readily at maturity, and appears as naked, egg-shaped, tiny grains (approximately 1/35 inch long).

Stinkgrass, introduced from the old world, is found throughout the United States. It is common in waste places, gardens, alfalfa and other crops. More than one species is reported to occur in the western U.S.

Non-standard names: lovegrass and candy-grass.

Below the leaf at the stem juncture is a fringe of straight hairs.

Many egg-shaped seeds are contained in these multifloreted spikelets of stinkgrass.

451

Southwestern cupgrass
Eriochloa gracilis (Fourn.) A.S. Hitchc.

Southwestern cupgrass
Poaceae
(Grass family)

This is an annual, 1 to 3 feet tall, that reproduces by seed and by prostrate stems that root at the nodes. The inflorescence is pubescent, 2 to 6 inches long, with short, erect to spreading branches that are 1 to 2 inches long. Spikelets, 1/4 to 3/16 inch long, having scattered hairs, and tapering into a point at the tip, and a darkened cup-like ring around the base. Seed is oval, flat on one side and rounded on the other, about 1/3 inch long, and has a short point at the tip.

Seedlings look similar to large crabgrass (*Digitaria sanguinalis* (L.) Scop.) and can be distinguished by the lighter green color and absence of hairs. A second species, prairie cupgrass (*E. contracta* A.S. Hitchc.), looks similar to southwestern cupgrass and can be distinguished by pubescent leaf blades and awned florets. Both species are native grasses and can be found in the Southwest.

During seedling stage, southwestern cupgrass resembles large crabgrass and can be distinguished by having bright green leaves and no pubescence.

Spikelets, found in spikes 1 to 2 inches long, have a darkened ring around the base.

Tall fescue
Festuca arundinacea Schreb.

Tall fescue
Poaceae
(Grass family)

Tall fescue is a deep-rooted, tufted, long-lived perennial with few to many seed stalks up to 4 feet tall. Leaves numerous, stiff, flat to somewhat rolled, dark green. The panicles are 4 to 12 inches long.

Introduced from Europe as a forage species, tall fescue is widely cultivated as a seed and forage crop and is found on roadsides and dry waste areas.

The contracted panicle of tall fescue is a good identification characteristic.

Stems and leaves are smooth and have a glossy appearance.

Common velvetgrass
Holcus lanatus L.

Common velvetgrass
Poaceae
(Grass family)

A perennial up to 3 feet tall with stems that are closely clustered. The entire plant is more or less grayish and velvety. Leaves are broad, long and pointed at the apex. Flower panicles, 3 to 6 inches long, are plume-like, dense, pale-green to purplish and hairy. The second floret of each spikelet possesses a small curved, hook-like awn.

German velvetgrass (*H. mollis* L.) is a perennial with a spreading rootstock. It is greener and less hairy, stems are hairy only at the nodes. The awn of the second floret is bent but not hooked. Both grasses are native to Europe.

Non-standard names: Yorkshire fog for common velvetgrass, creeping velvetgrass for German velvetgrass.

The stems of common velvetgrass (right) are pubescent for their entire length while those of German velvetgrass (left) are only pubescent at the nodes.

Rhizomes of German velvetgrass are densely matted, therefore excluding other vegetation.

457

Foxtail barley
Hordeum jubatum L.

Foxtail barley and squirreltail
Poaceae
(Grass family)

Foxtail barley is a perennial that reproduces by seed. Plants grow 1 to 2 feet tall and produce a pale green, bushy, spike. Leaf blades are 1/8 to 1/4 inch wide; the sheaths may vary from smooth to densely hairy. At maturity the heads break into 7-awned clusters consisting of 3 spikelets (1 fertile and 2 sterile). Spikelets are 1-flowered. Awns are 1 to 2 1/2 inches long.

Squirreltail, *Elymus elymoides* (Rafin) Swezey, is a related perennial grass with open spikes and long, minutely-barbed awns. The most obvious difference between the 2 genera is the fact that *Sitanion* has 2 or more florets per spikelet, and 2 spikelets per node. Foxtail barley is a native of North America, and is especially common in wet or alkaline soils, and rundown meadows and pastures. Squirreltail is more common on dry hills, plains, open woods or rocky slopes. Both foxtail barley and squirreltail are palatable to livestock at younger stages; but awns of mature plants can cause serious injury to animals' eyes, nose, throat and ears. At least 4 species of *Elymus* are considered weedy and at least 7 species of *Hordeum* (in addition to barley) are reported to occur in the West.

Once established, plants are blue-green in color, and appear as clumps.

Squirreltail resembles foxtail, but has open spikes with long, minutely-barbed awns.

Hare barley
Hordeum leporinum Link

Hare barley
Poaceae
(Grass family)

Annual up to 10 inches tall. Leaf blades are 1/16 to 3/16 inch wide and smooth to hairy. Auricles at base of blade are well developed. Inflorescence a spike 1/2 to 4 inches long with awns 1/4 to 1 inch long.

Foxtail barley (*H. jubatum* L.) does not have auricles and Mediterranean barley (*H. hystrix* Roth) may have one small auricle. Hare barley was introduced from southern Europe and is a common weed of cropland and waste areas in most western states. Awns of mature plants can cause serious injury to eyes, nose, and throat of grazing animals.

Non-standard name: wild barley.

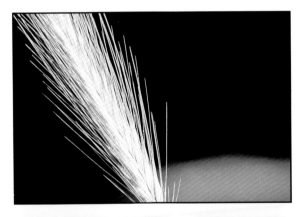

The conspicuous awns of hare barley are typical of the wild Hordeum.

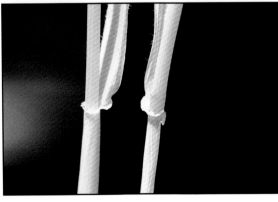

The well developed clasping auricles are easily observed on hare barley.

461

Mexican sprangletop
Leptochloa uninervia (Presl) Hitchc. & Chase

Mexican sprangletop
Poaceae
(Grass family)

An erect or spreading often reddish or purplish annual 1 to 3 feet high. Leaf blades are thin and flat, 1/4 to 1/3 inch wide and up to 12 inches long. The central nerve of the leaf is nearly white, giving the leaf a 1-nerved appearance from which the species name is derived. Spikelets are grouped to form a loose, fine-textured panicle. Mature spikelets are no more than 1/4 inch long and are lead colored.

Bearded sprangletop (*L. fascicularis* (Lam.) Gray) is similar to Mexican sprangletop but has awned spikelets. Red sprangletop (*L. filiformis* (Lam.) Beauv.) is also a similar species having a reddish panicle, often as long as 18 inches. Mexican, bearded, and red sprangletop occur in southwestern United States. They grow particularly well in wet areas at the edges of fields, irrigation and drainage canals. They are also troublesome summer annual weeds in irrigated crops. Mexican sprangletop is also called *Megastachya uninervia* Presl.

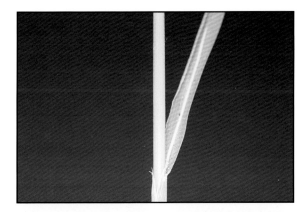

This leaf of Mexican sprangletop illustrates its prominent central nerve.

Red sprangletop has a large, reddish, open panicle.

Italian ryegrass
Lolium multiflorum Lam.

Italian ryegrass
Poaceae
(Grass family)

An upright annual, often purplish at the base, from 1 to 2 1/2 feet tall. Leaves are shiny and have flat blades 1/8 to 1/4 inch wide, dark green with prominent veins. Spikes are terminal and flat with spikelets that are placed edgewise and alternate along the flowering stem. The spikes are often as long as 12 inches.

Italian ryegrass was introduced from Europe and is a common weed of road-sides, waste areas and cultivated crops. It is used as a temporary turf before establishing lawns and as a temporary pasture grass.

Non-standard name: annual ryegrass.

Leaves have small clasping auricles, are smooth, shiny and have prominent veins.

The flat terminal spikes have spikelets that alternate along the stem.

Witchgrass

Panicum capillare L.

Witchgrass
Poaceae
(Grass family)

Witchgrass is an annual, soft and hairy throughout, 1 to 2 feet tall, reproducing by seed. Leaf blades are 1/8 to 9/16 inch wide. Spikelets form a large open panicle with many stiff branches, each bearing a single, small, shiny, green or grayish seed at the tip.

Witchgrass is a common weed found along roadsides, waste places, cultivated fields, depleted hayland and ranges in poor condition. It may become a nuisance in cultivated fields with poorly established crops. It does not compete well with established perennial grasses, therefore, it is not a serious problem on ranges in good condition. Witchgrass is somewhat palatable before seedheads develop, but is worthless once it matures, and lowers hay quality. When mature the whole plant breaks away, scattering seed as it tumbles across the land.

Non-standard name: ticklegrass.

All vegetative parts of this plant are extremely hairy. Leaves are often 1/2 inch wide on immature plants.

Witchgrass has a large open panicle with many stiff branches, each bearing a single seed.

Fall panicum
Panicum dichotomiflorum Michx.

Fall panicum
Poaceae
(Grass family)

An annual with an upright or spreading growth habit, up to 3 feet tall from a bent or twisted base. Leaf blades are up to 3/4 inch wide, usually with a prominent white midrib. Ligule is a dense ring of white hairs up to 1/16 inch long. Open panicles are both terminal and axillary.

A native of central and eastern North America, it has now spread to the West. It is an aggressive, widespread weed of cropland in the East.

Non-standard name: western witchgrass.

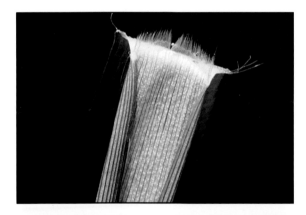

The ligule consists of a dense ring of white hairs.

The partially emerged seedhead of fall panicum has individual seeds at the ends of the branches.

469

Wild-proso millet

Panicum miliaceum L.

Wild-proso millet
Poaceae
(Grass family)

Wild-proso millet is an annual, 2 to 6 feet tall, with erect stems that branch at the base. Leaf blades are hairy, 1/2 to 3/4 inch wide; sheaths open with long spreading hairs. The ligule is a fringe of dense hairs 1/16 inch long that are fused at the base. The inflorescence is a spreading panicle 6 to 12 inches wide and not fully extended from the leaf sheath. Spikelets are 2-flowered, the upper floret is fertile, the lower is sterile. Glumes are 1/8 inch long, ovate, pointed at the tip and strongly nerved. Seeds are smooth, shiny, olive brown to black. Seedlings can often be identified by the attached seed coat on the roots.

The exact origin of wild-proso millet is not known; however, it may have come from Asia or central Europe. Wild-proso millet is a prolific seed producer and a vigorous competitor in row crops. The seed can be spread by harvesting equipment, uncomposted manure, birds, small animals and irrigation water. Infestations often start at field entrances or along roadsides, so careful attention should be paid to these areas to prevent establishment. Flowering and seed production occur from July to September.

Seedlings are hairy with wide leaves. Careful removal from the soil often exposes the characteristic black undeteriorated seed.

Seed color, ranging from olive brown to black, is the only positive identification characteristic distinguishing wild-proso millet from domestic proso millet (which has yellow or light brown seed as shown in lower right corner of photo).

Dallisgrass
Paspalum dilatatum Poir.

Dallisgrass
Poaceae
(Grass family)

A perennial, 1/2 to 5 feet high, originating from a hard, knotty base, that reproduces only by seed. Leaf blades are flat, 2 to 6 inches long and 1/4 to 1/2 inch wide. The inflorescence consists of 3 to 5 narrow branches which are 1 to 3 inches long and alternate along the upper part of the flowering stem. Spikelets are about 1/8 inch long and form an even row along one side of the spike. The seed is yellowish, about 1/8 inch long and circular.

Dallisgrass is a native of South America and can be found in the southwestern United States in moist areas such as irrigated pastures, turf and ornamental groundcovers.

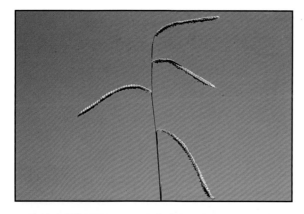

Flower stems of dallisgrass are branched with spikelets arranged on one side.

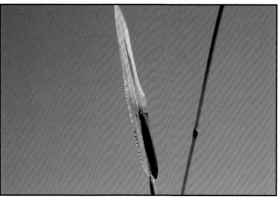

Dallisgrass leaves are flat, smooth and without hairs or auricles and are produced in abundance at the base of the plant.

Kikuyugrass
Pennisetum clandestinum Hochst. ex Chiov.

Kikuyugrass
Poaceae
(Grass family)

A prostrate perennial which grows rapidly, particularly during the summer months, spreading from rhizomes and stolons. Leaves vary from 1 to 6 inches in length and 1/8 to 1/2 inch in width with a collar of upright bristles where the leaf blade joins the stem. The flowers are borne inconspicuously at the stem nodes. However, filamentous anthers are produced in the early morning and appear above the surface of the turf, giving a whitish cast to the area.

Kikuyugrass is an introduced species from East Africa and is commonly a weed problem in turf, groundcover and along ditchbanks in the coastal regions of California and Hawaii. Flowering begins in March and continues through October.

Stolon of kikuyugrass.

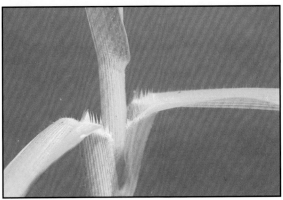

Leaves of kikuyugrass contain upright bristles within the collar.

Reed canarygrass
Phalaris arundinacea L.

Reed canarygrass
Poaceae
(Grass family)

Stout perennial that regenerates from large rootstocks, with stems 2 to 7 feet tall that are covered with a waxy coating that gives it a blue-green color. Leaf blades are flat, 1/4 to 3/4 inch wide. The panicle is more or less compact at first, then the branches spread.

This aggressive species is found on wet ground, along streams and in marshes in all of the western states. It is especially a problem when growing in canals and irrigation ditches.

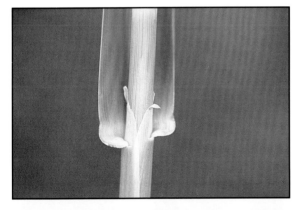

Ligules of reed canarygrass surround the stem, auricles are somewhat blunt.

Panicles are initially compact (top) but open fully at maturity (bottom).

Littleseed canarygrass
Phalaris minor Retz.

Littleseed canarygrass
Poaceae
(Grass family)

Erect winter annual, 1/2 to 3 feet tall, with bluish-green foliage and weak stems that are bent at the base. Leaves are flat or folded, 1/4 to 1/2 inch wide, 10 to 18 inches in length. Flowering head short, thick and oblong, 1 to 3 inches in length. Spikelets densely crowded and overlapping in the heads. Glumes surrounding the spikelet are sharply pointed and sharply folded. Shiny straw-colored seeds are egg-shaped, pointed at the tip and about 1/8 inch long.

Littleseed canarygrass is a native of the Mediterranean and can be found in barley, wheat, seedling alfalfa and other winter-cultivated crops in California and Arizona. It flowers in April and May.

Non-standard name: canarygrass.

Heads are 1 to 3 inches long and composed of densely crowded, overlapping spikelets.

Young seedlings often exude a red pigment or "blood" when broken at the base.

Annual bluegrass
Poa annua L.

Annual bluegrass
Poaceae
(Grass family)

Annual with more or less flattened stems that are spreading or erect. The stems are from 2 to 12 inches long, sometimes forming dense clumps. The leaves are bright green and soft with the tip curved and prow-like. The inflorescences are more or less pyramidal, the branches spreading.

This native of Europe is found throughout the western states. It thrives in lawns, gardens, cultivated crops, roadsides, and other open areas. Annual bluegrass can be especially troublesome in lawns where it tends to grow faster than other grasses and once mature it dies, resulting in brown spots in the lawn. It is commonly found as an impurity of lawn grass seed, and is a weed for grass seed producers. The flowering and seed production period is March to August.

The inflorescence of annual bluegrass showing pyramidal shape with spreading branches.

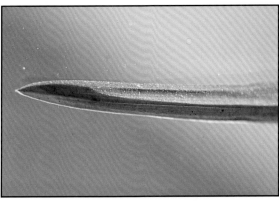

Leaf blades are curved upward on the edges and tip, giving them a canoe shape.

Bulbous bluegrass
Poa bulbosa L.

Bulbous bluegrass
Poaceae
(Grass family)

A perennial that grows from basal bulbs, the culms closely clustered, 1/2 to 2 feet tall. Leaf blades are narrow, flat or loosely rolled; with membranous ligules about 1/8 inch long. Flowers are usually modified to bulblets with a dark purple base.

Introduced from Europe, bulbous bluegrass is now weedy in pastures, grain fields and roadsides in scattered areas of most states in the West.

Panicles produce flowers which are modified into propagative bulblets.

Bulbs are found at the base of mature bulbous bluegrass plants.

Rabbitfoot polypogon
Polypogon monspeliensis (L.) Desf.

Rabbitfoot polypogon
Poaceae
(Grass family)

An erect or prostrate-based, shallow-rooted, annual grass growing 1/2 to 2 feet tall. Leaves are narrow and often abruptly bent. Large, soft, pale green, spike-like panicles somewhat resemble the shape of a furry rabbit foot, hence the common name.

Rabbitfoot polypogon is an introduced species native to Eurasia and Africa that has become widely distributed in the United States. It is often found along roadsides, waterways, and marshy or saline waste areas. It can become a problem in pastures and lawns.

Non-standard name: rabbitfoot grass.

Large "furry" seedheads somewhat resemble the shape of a rabbit's foot.

The leaf sheath, leaf blade, and collar region are useful identification characteristics of the plant.

485

Hardgrass
Sclerochloa dura (L.) Beauv.

Hardgrass
Poaceae
(Grass family)

A low-growing annual with many prostrate to erect stems 1 to 5 inches long. Foliage is gray-green in color, with leaf blades generally flat. Membranous ligules are pronounced, but somewhat variable in shape. Sheaths remain open for approximately one-half the length of the leaf. Inflorescences are somewhat one-sided clusters of spikelets, often partly enclosed by the upper leaf sheath.

Hardgrass is a European native which has become a serious lawn and turf weed in many parts of the U.S. It is common in disturbed waste areas.

Non-standard name: tufted hardgrass.

Typical inflorescence showing light-colored margins of blunt-tipped florets.

The flattened leaf sheath has a pronounced, pointed, membranous ligule.

Cereal rye
Secale cereale L.

Cereal rye
Poaceae
(Grass family)

An annual, or occasionally biennial, 18 to 40 inches tall. Leaf blades flat, 1/16 to 3/8 inch wide, rough, at least above, with open sheaths, usually with well-developed auricles, and a membranous ligule. Leaf sheaths may be hairy or smooth. The inflorescence is a terminal spike, somewhat flattened, and often with short awns.

This is the domestic cereal rye grown widely throughout North America. However, field contamination from volunteer rye often creates a serious problem for wheat producers. When rye escapes cultivation it can become established on roadsides, waste places, and even open rangeland.

Synonym: common rye.

Flattened 2-sided seedheads have short awns.

Leaf sheaths of common rye may be smooth or hairy and have auricles that are usually well developed.

489

Yellow foxtail
Setaria glauca (L.) Beauv.

Yellow foxtail and green foxtail
Poaceae
(Grass family)

Yellow foxtail is a tufted annual, 1 to 3 feet tall, with erect stems that branch at the base. The leaf blade is smooth, 1/8 to 3/8 inch wide with distinct hairs on leaf margins near the base. Leaf sheath smooth, 2 to 8 inches long and 1/2 inch wide. Panicles cylindrical, with crowded spikelets that are subtended by 6 to 10 long yellowish bristles. Seeds are broadly oval, green to yellow to dark brown, coarsely roughened and approximately 1/8 inch long.

Green foxtail (*Setaria viridis* (L.) Beauv.) is generally shorter in height with roughened leaf sheaths, without hairs, and has much smaller seeds.

These plants are native to Eurasia, but common throughout most of North America (green foxtail is more common than yellow foxtail in the western U.S.). They are often serious problems in spring-seeded alfalfa, row crops, and small grain crops, but they also occur along roadsides and in waste areas. These plants are responsible for reductions in yield, increased cleaning costs, and expensive control measures. Flowering and seed production occur July to September.

Non-standard name: pigeongrass.

Prior to seedhead emergence, yellow foxtail and green foxtail look identical, except that yellow foxtail has numerous long hairs at the base of the leaf.

Green foxtail's spike-like panicles range from 1 to 4 inches long with crowded spikelets.

491

Bristly foxtail
Setaria verticillata (L.) Beauv.

Bristly foxtail
Poaceae
(Grass family)

An annual, 1 to 3 feet tall. Leaf blades flat, 3/16 to 1/2 inch wide, smooth or with a few hairs near the base on the upper surface, having open sheaths and lacking auricles, with a ligule of hairs or a hair-fringed membrane. The inflorescence is a spike-like panicle that appears somewhat segmented or interrupted. Spikelets are subtended by long scabrous bristles that remain attached to the rachis after seeds drop.

Bristly foxtail, a native of Eurasia and Africa, closely resembles green foxtail when in the vegetative growth stage. The primary difference between this and other *Setaria* species is the fact that minute barbs on the stiff bristles of *S. verticillata* are oriented downward, causing seedheads to cling strongly to clothing and animals.

Non-standard name: bur bristlegrass.

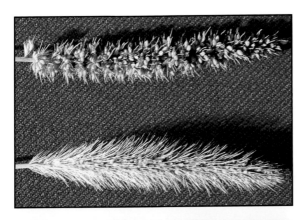

Comparisons of bristly foxtail (top) and green foxtail seedheads.

Notice the open leaf sheath and hairy ligule of bristly foxtail.

493

Johnsongrass
Sorghum halepense (L.) Pers.

Johnsongrass
Poaceae
(Grass family)

Johnsongrass is a vigorous perennial plant resembling forage sorghum that spreads by seed or by creeping, robust fleshy rhizomes. Erect stems are generally solid, have prominent nodes, and grow 2 to 8 feet tall. Leaf blades are flat with conspicuous midveins, and are often as much as 1 inch wide. Ligules are short and membranous, with a terminal fringe of fine hairs. Mature inflorescence is a large open panicle bearing many awn-tipped, shiny, reddish to purple spikelets. Awns are bent and needle-like, and not all spikelets have awns.

Johnsongrass was introduced from the Mediterranean region as a hay or forage crop. Once thought of as strictly a warm season grass, it has adapted and can be found in most of the western states. Plants form hydrocyanic acid when under frost or moisture stress, making the plant toxic to livestock.

Shattercane (*S. bicolor* (L.) Moench) is an annual that often becomes a nuisance in cultivated fields. It probably developed from outcrosses of cultivated sorghum and Johnsongrass.

Mature panicles or seedheads bear many awn-tipped, shiny, purplish spikelets.

A common method of propagation is from large fleshy rhizomes in addition to seed.

495

Medusahead

Taeniatherum caput-medusae (L.) Nevski

Medusahead
Poaceae
(Grass family)

An aggressive winter annual 6 to 24 inches tall. Leaf blades more or less rolled, generally 1/8 inch wide or less. Inflorescence a long-awned spike that is nearly as wide as long. Mature awns twisted, 1 to 4 inches long, stiff, and minutely barbed.

Flowering and seed formation occur in May and June. Sometimes confused with foxtail barley or squirreltail, medusahead can be distinguished by the fact that its spike or head does not break apart as seeds mature and that it is an annual. Instead, individual awned-florets fall away, leaving a bristly head made up of awn-like glumes that will persist over winter. Medusahead seedlings appear similar to downy brome, except the latter is much hairier.

Medusahead, introduced from Eurasia, is predominant on millions of acres of semi-arid rangeland in the Pacific Northwest. It is extremely competitive, crowding out even such undesirable species as downy brome. Infested ranches have suffered 40 to 75 percent reductions in grazing capacity. Control of small isolated infestations is critical.

Non-standard name: medusahead rye.

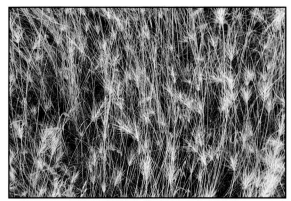

Medusahead is a highly competitive plant that crowds out all other vegetation on infested rangeland.

Twisted awns or beards are a good identification characteristic of medusahead.

497

Ventenata
Ventenata dubia [Leers] Gross. & Dur.

Ventenata
Poaceae
(Grass family)

A slender erect annual, 6 to 27 inches tall. Leaves rolled lengthways or folded, narrow, 3/4 to 2 3/8 inches long, sheaths open, ligules membranous, cut into narrow segments. Inflorescence a more or less lax, open, pyramidal panicle, to 8 inches long, tawny to light yellow, with a distinct sheen. Spikelets are 7/16 to 5/8 inch long, near the ends of long branches; lowest floret is sharp-pointed to short-awned, the awns to 3/16 inch long, straight. The awns on the upper florets are 3/8 to 1 inch long, bent and twisted.

A Eurasian species, ventenata occurs in grain crops, rangeland and disturbed sites. Cattle will not graze it once the panicles emerge.

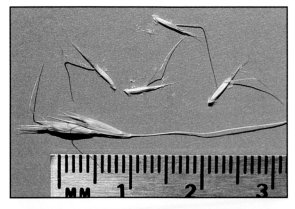

The upper florets in a ventenata spikelet have bent awns and a hairy callus.

Spikelets are 7/16 to 5/8 inch long, near the ends of long branches.

Rattail fescue
Vulpia myuros (L.) K.C. Gmel.

Rattail fescue
Poaceae
(Grass family)

An annual up to 25 inches tall. Leaf blades are folded and less than 1/16 inch wide. The sheaths and blades are hairless. The panicles are narrow and up to 8 inches long. Florets have awns which are 5/16 to 3/8 inch long.

Introduced from Europe and irregularly scattered in the West in wasteland, fields, and in overgrazed areas. Rattail fescue is sometimes referred to as *Festuca myuros* L.

A seedling of rattail fescue; notice the narrow, tightly folded leaves.

The narrow, awned panicles of rattail fescue are a useful identification characteristic.

Prostrate knotweed
Polygonum aviculare L.

Prostrate knotweed and silversheath knotweed
Polygonaceae
(Buckwheat family)

Prostrate annual, 1 to 3 feet tall, with wiry corrugated stems that are enlarged at each joint. Leaves are hairless, alternate and lance-shaped to oblong, 1/2 to 2 1/2 inches long and 1/8 to 1/3 inch wide with silvery papery sheaths at each node. Flowers are small and pink, occurring in clusters along the flower stems at leaf axils. Flowering stems compose about half of the height of a mature plant. The seed is about 1/16 inch long, 3-angled and reddish-brown.

Silversheath knotweed (*Polygonum argyrocoleon* Steud. ex Kunze) was probably introduced from central Asia and is a weed in croplands, horticultural and ornamental production areas in Arizona and California. It flowers in late winter and early summer.

Prostrate knotweed has small pinkish flowers borne in leaf axils.

Silversheath knotweed has showy papery sheaths at the axil of each leaf.

Wild buckwheat
Polygonum convolvulus L.

Wild buckwheat
Polygonaceae
(Buckwheat family)

An annual weed with stems trailing along the ground, often twining about other plants. Leaves are heart-shaped with a tapered point, and are arranged alternately along the stem. An inconspicuous papery sheath encircles the stem at the base of each leaf petiole. Clusters of tiny greenish flowers are borne in leaf axils. Seeds are triangular, dull black, slightly roughened and about 3/16 inch long.

Wild buckwheat was introduced from Europe, and is now a common weed in cultivated fields, gardens, orchards and non-crop areas of our region. Superficially resembling field bindweed, wild buckwheat can be distinguished by its annual habit, pointed leaves, papery leaf sheaths and small green flowers. (Bindweed flowers are white to lavender, large, showy and trumpet-shaped.)

Seedling plants have distinctive heart-shaped leaves.

Clusters of greenish flowers are borne in leaf axils. Each flower produces a hard, triangular black seed.

505

Japanese knotweed
Polygonum cuspidatum Sieb. & Zucc.

Japanese knotweed
Polygonaceae
(Buckwheat family)

Perennial from long creeping rhizomes. Stems are stout, reddish-brown, 4 to 9 feet tall, woody but die back at end of growing season. The nodes are slightly swollen and surrounded by thin papery sheaths. Leaves are short-petioled, broadly ovate, 2 to 6 inches long and about two-thirds as wide, narrowed to a point. The flowers are greenish white to cream, borne in large plume-like clusters at ends of stems and in leaf axils. The fruit is 3-sided, black and shiny.

Introduced from Asia as an ornamental, now escaped to become a weed of roadsides, waste areas, ditchbanks, and pastures.

Non-standard name: fleeceflower.

Small flowers are grouped in plume-like clusters at ends of stems and in leaf axils.

Leaves are short-petioled and broadly ovate, 2 to 6 inches long.

Erect knotweed
Polygonum erectum L.

Prostrate knotweed and erect knotweed
Polygonaceae
(Buckwheat family)

Extremely variable annuals with wiry stems. Nodes are somewhat swollen, often surrounded with the torn remnant of a short, papery leaf sheath. Leaves are generally lance-shaped, blue-green and alternate. Inconspicuous, greenish-white flowers are borne in the leaf axils.

Several species occur in the Western region. The basal branches of prostrate knotweed *(P. aviculare* L.) become prostrate, while erect knotweed *(P. erectum)* is more upright. Erect and prostrate knotweeds are natives of the Old World, but are now distributed throughout North America. They can become a problem in irrigated and dryland crops, as well as in waste areas and other non-crop sites. Prostrate knotweed seems to thrive in dry compacted soils.

Non-standard name: devil's shoestring, wireweed.

Prostrate knotweed lies flat on the soil surface; erect knotweed is upright.

In erect and prostrate knotweeds inconspicuous greenish-white flowers are borne in leaf axils.

Pale smartweed

Polygonum lapathifolium L.

Pale smartweed and ladysthumb
Polygonaceae
(Buckwheat family)

Annual weeds, with erect or spreading stems usually 1 to 3 feet long. Stems may initiate roots at lower nodes. Leaves are alternate, narrow, lance-shaped, often marked with a characteristic pink or purplish "lady's thumbprint" near the middle. Leaf nodes are conspicuous and sheathed, as is common with most members of this genus. Flowers are small, pink or rose-colored; they are borne in dense, erect, terminal and axillary spikes approximately 1 inch long. Pale smartweed, *(P. lapathifolium* L.), and ladysthumb (*Polygonum persicaria* L.) are similar in appearance, but may be differentiated by the fact that ladysthumb sheaths are tipped with short bristles, while those of pale smartweed lack bristles. Pale smartweed spikes tend to be longer, and the flowers a lighter pink. Ladysthumb seeds are shiny, black, and may be either flattened or 3-angled. Pale smartweed seeds are flattened, shiny and brown.

These amphibious species are often found in wet or moist undisturbed sites, but they can also become troublesome in cultivated fields and irrigated pastures. Several other species also occur in our region. Other related species resembling ladysthumb include swamp smartweed (*P. coccineum* Muhl. ex Willd.) and water smartweed (*P. amphibium* L.).

Ladysthumb leaves have a darkened area near the center of the leaves. Pale smartweed leaves are consistent in color.

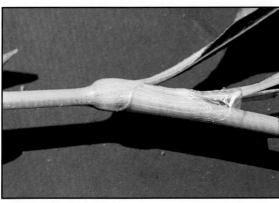

Smartweed leaf sheaths are very apparent, clear membranes.

Red sorrel
Rumex acetosella L.

Red sorrel
Polygonaceae
(Buckwheat family)

Perennial with slender creeping rootstocks. Stem somewhat woody at the base, 1/2 to 2 feet tall, little branched. Blade of the lower leaves somewhat arrow-shaped with 1 or 2 conspicuous basal lobes. Upper leaves are more slender and sometimes without basal lobes. The slender petiole has a papery sheath at point of attachment to stem. Leaves and stems have a sour taste. Flowers are borne in branched terminal clusters. The plants are dioecious, the male flowers are orange-yellow and the female flowers are red-orange. The fruits are small, 3-angled, enclosed in 3 reddish, persistent flower parts. The triangular seeds are polished mahogany colored.

Red sorrel is native to Europe and can be found throughout the West. While apparently thriving on acid soils, it has adapted to other soils and various growing conditions and often occurs in lawns, fields, gardens, and along roadsides.

Non-standard name: sheep sorrel.

Small reddish flowers are found on flower stalks up to 2 feet long.

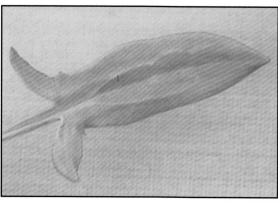

Arrowhead-shaped leaves have lobes at base of blade.

Curly dock
Rumex crispus L.

Curly dock
Polygonaceae
(Buckwheat family)

A robust tap-rooted perennial growing 2 to 5 feet tall. Stems are erect, generally unbranched on the lower half, often reddish and slightly ridged. Leaves are mostly basal, with curly or wavy margins, elongated, 4 to 12 inches long and lack hairs. Flowers are small and in dense, green, spike-like, terminal and axillary clusters. Inflorescences and even entire plants turn reddish-brown at maturity. Individual seeds are enclosed in a papery, sometimes corky, winged structure, 1/8 to 3/16 inch long, that facilitates distribution by wind or water.

Broadleaf dock (*R. obtusifolius* L.) can be distinguished by its broader leaves and the presence of 1 to 3 spines on the wing structure of the fruit. *Rumex* species are native to Eurasia. They are especially common in wet meadows, along ditchbanks and in waste areas.

Non-standard names: sour dock and yellow dock.

The wide leaf of broadleaf dock.

The spined wing structure of broadleaf dock fruits (right) compared to the smooth wing margins of curly dock (left).

Western brackenfern
Pteridium aquilinum var. *pubescens* Underw.

Western brackenfern
Dennstaedtiaceae
(Fern family)

Coarse, medium-sized to large perennial ferns, 1 1/2 to 6 feet tall, with branched, creeping, woody rhizomes. Fronds are leathery, pinnate to decompound and densely hairy on the underside. Brown spores are borne along the undersurface edge of each frond segment, and are protected by a narrowly inrolled indusial leaf margin. Newly emerging unrolled fronds appear as fiddlenecks in the spring.

Pteridium is distinguished from other fern genera primarily by the fact that its rhizomes have no scales. Other genera will have scales, or scales and hairs on rhizomes. Brackenfern is a native species found throughout most of the western U.S. It is most likely to occur in open woods or mountains where soil pH is neutral or acidic. It is not generally considered aggressive, but it is included for its potential to cause livestock poisoning. Poisoning in horses and sheep appears to be cumulative, and symptoms may not be evident until some time after initial feeding. A second variety without hair, eastern brackenfern *(Pteridium aquilinum* var. *latiusculum* (Desv.) Underw.), is also found in Colorado and Wyoming.

Synonym of Dennstaedtiaceae: Polypodiaceae.

Fronds (fern leaves) have a knobby appearance in early spring as they develop.

The underside of compound fronds are hairy, developing reddish-brown reproductive spores in late summer.

517

Desert rockpurslane
Calandrinia ciliata (R. & P.) DC. var *menziesii* (Hook.) Macbr.

Desert rockpurslane
Portulacaceae
(Purslane family)

Annual somewhat fleshy plant with low and spreading to more or less erect stems. The leaves are narrow and strap-shaped. Flowers are borne in axils of upper leaves and have petals that are rose-red or rarely white. Seeds are numerous, black and shiny.

A native species found in areas that are moist, at least in the spring; it often becomes weedy in cultivated fields and orchards.

Non-standard name: redmaids.

Narrow, strap-shaped leaves of a seedling rosette help in early identification.

Flowers have 5 petals (usually red), 2 sepals, 5 to 12 stamen and 3 stigmas.

Miner's lettuce
Montia perfoliata (Donn) T.J. Howell

Miner's lettuce
Portulacaceae
(Purslane family)

A low fleshy annual with basal leaves varying from narrow and strap-shaped to those which are long-petioled, and broad-bladed. Pairs of stem leaves unite around the stem to form a rounded or 2-angled disk below the white or pink flowers.

This species is widely distributed in the West. It is usually found in moist, shady areas.

A pair of leaves unite around the stem to form a 2-angled disk below the flower.

Two leaf types include the circular leaf pairs below the flowers and ovate singular leaves.

Common purslane
Portulaca oleracea L.

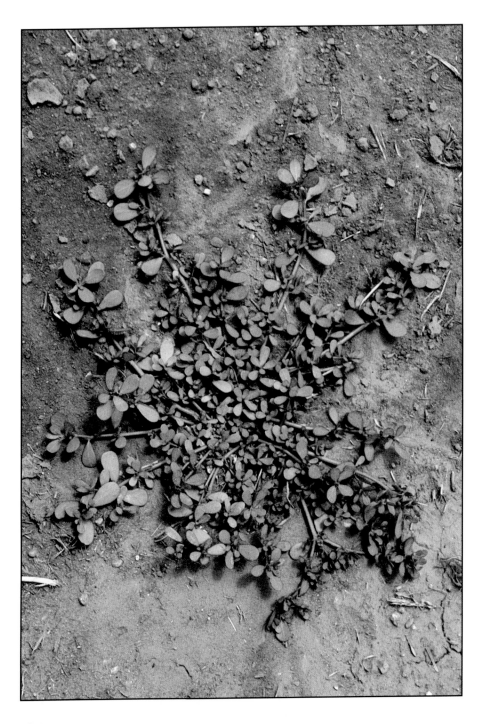

Common purslane
Portulacaceae
(Purslane family)

A fleshy, prostrate annual with smooth reddish or flesh-colored stems. Branches radiating from a central rooting point reach lengths in excess of 12 inches and form dense vegetative mats. Smooth, shiny, succulent leaves are somewhat teardrop-shaped, wider at the tip than at the base. Five-petalled yellow flowers are borne singly in leaf axils, and open only in sunshine. Numerous, tiny, black seeds are produced in capsules resembling the flower buds.

Introduced from Europe, common purslane has become a troublesome weed in cultivated fields and gardens. It is especially persistent in soils that remain moist much of the time. Production of seed throughout the growing season, and the ability to root again after cultivation make this plant especially difficult to control. Seeds can remain dormant in the soil for years before germinating. Purslane has limited value as a potherb, but is rarely eaten.

Leaves and stems are fleshy with small yellow flowers appearing in leaf axils in late summer.

Seedlings of purslane have teardrop-shaped succulent leaves that are wider at the tip than at the base.

523

Geyer larkspur
Delphinium geyeri Greene

Geyer larkspur
Ranunculaceae
(Buttercup family)

Geyer Larkspur is a perennial with hollow stems that grows up to 2 feet tall and with tuberous woody roots. Leaves are finely divided, lobed into 3 to 5 divisions that are lobed again. Flowers, terminal, purple, with a distinct spur pointing backwards; seeds borne in an upright pod.

Geyer larkspur is native to the Rocky Mountain region and is common on western rangelands in the plains and mountain areas. It is similar in appearance to tall larkspur but may be distinguished by its smaller, more finely divided leaves. It flowers in the spring, grows in lower elevations, and is smaller in height. Toxic alkaloids cause fatal poisoning in cattle, whereas sheep and horses are rarely affected. It is rarely eaten after it reaches maturity in late June. Cattle losses may be reduced by keeping them off infested ranges until other forage is available, grazing with sheep before allowing cattle to graze, or by treating with herbicides. When using herbicides, special precautions must be taken to keep cattle off treated areas, because plants may become more palatable following treatments.

Early spring growth of geyer larkspur is the most poisonous to cattle and is one of the first rangeland plants to appear in spring.

Flowers, connected to the main stem by pedicels, have 4 less conspicuous petals and 5 sepals with a spur on their back sides.

525

Low larkspur
Delphinium nuttallianum Pritz. ex Walp.

Low larkspur
Ranunculaceae
(Buttercup family)

A simple, rarely branched perennial, typically reaching 10 to 20 inches in height, arising from a shallow, clustered, tuberous root system. Leaves are deeply parted into linear finger-like lobes. Large showy flowers are blue-purple or sometimes pale blue to white, with prominent spurs. Normally 3 spreading, beaked, seed follicles form from each flower.

Low larkspur is widespread throughout the West. It is listed by some authors as *D. menziesii* DC. and *D. nelsonii* Greene. At least 20 species or varieties of *Delphinium* are reported in the western U.S. Like many other members of the genus, low larkspur is poisonous to livestock.

Violet, lavender, or white spurred flowers each produce 3 beaked seed follicles.

Leaves are 3- to 5-parted with finger-like lobes.

527

Duncecap larkspur
Delphinium occidentale (Wats.) Wats.

Duncecap larkspur
Ranunculaceae
(Buttercup family)

A hollow-stemmed perennial up to 5 feet tall from woody tuberous roots. Leaves are large, dissected, alternate, lobed into 3 to 5 divisions that are lobed again. Flowers, in terminal racemes, purple, with a distinct spur pointing backwards. Seeds are borne in an upright pod.

It is native to the Rocky Mountain region and may be distinguished from geyer larkspur (*D. geyeri* Greene) because it grows at higher elevations, is usually much taller, has larger leaves and stems, and flowers in the summer instead of spring. All parts of the plant including seeds contain toxic alkaloids. Fatal poisoning occurs mainly in cattle, whereas losses rarely occur in sheep and horses. Cattle losses may be minimized by keeping them off larkspur infested ranges until other forage is available, grazing the area with sheep before allowing cattle to graze, or by treating with herbicides. When using herbicides special precautions must be taken to keep cattle off treated areas, since applications of some herbicides increase the palatability of larkspur.

Leaves are alternate on stems. Each leaf is lobed into sections then individual sections are lobed again.

Purple flowers contain 5 sepals with a spur-like appendage pointing backwards. Each flower is connected to the stem by a pedicel.

529

Tall buttercup
Ranunculus acris L.

Tall buttercup
Ranunculaceae
(Buttercup family)

Hairy perennial, often reaching 3 feet in height, with stems much branched above. Lower leaves deeply 3- to 5-lobed, the lobes also deeply cut, upper leaves reduced and consisting of 3 to 4 narrow segments. Flowers yellow, 1 inch or more in diameter.

Spiny-fruited buttercup (*R. muricatus* L.) is an annual, 1/6 to 1 foot tall. Leafy branching stems single or clustered. Leaves petioled, blades 3- to 5-lobed, toothed. Fruit 1/4 inch or slightly longer with smooth border, stout curved beak, and generally spiny faces.

These species were introduced from Europe. Roughseed buttercup is common in the western United States, but tall buttercup is now well established throughout most of North America. Buttercup species usually occur in meadows and pastures and are generally avoided by livestock. Like other species of *Ranunculus*, tall buttercup has been reported to cause livestock poisonings.

Leaves of tall buttercup (right) and roughseed buttercup (left) are similar, with lobed and deeply cut margins.

Roughseed buttercup has 1/4 inch long fruit with a smooth border and spiny faces.

531

Creeping buttercup
Ranunculus repens L.

Creeping buttercup
Ranunculaceae
(Buttercup family)

Perennial that creeps and roots at the lower nodes of the hairy stems. Leaves are hairy with long petioles, the blades are 3-parted with toothed margins. Flower stems are long and erect; flowers are few and showy with yellow petals. Seedheads contain about 12 fruits, each about 1/8 inch long. Fruits are flattened and rounded, with a short backward-turned beak.

Creeping buttercup was introduced from Europe as an ornamental and now is considered weedy in moist locations. It is aggressive in pastures and is toxic to cattle.

The 3-parted leaf has toothed margins.

Buttercup flowers have 5 waxy petals, and mature into beaked fruits. Flowers are borne on long stalks.

533

Bur buttercup
Ranunculus testiculatus Crantz

Bur buttercup
Ranunculaceae
(Buttercup family)

A low-growing annual, 2 to 5 inches tall. Grayish-green leaves are basally attached, 1 to 4 inches long, with blades divided into finger-like segments. Yellow flowers, 5-petalled, develop into stiff brown burs about 1/2 to 3/4 inch in length.

Plants emerge, flower, and form fruit early in the spring, soon after snow-melt. Bur buttercup is a native of southeastern Europe. It has become a common weed in small grains, pastures, waste areas and along roadsides in several western states, including California, Oregon, Washington, Nevada, Utah, Idaho and Colorado. Bur buttercup can be competitive, especially in dryland small grain crops. It is highly toxic to sheep.

Non-standard names: little bur and testiculate buttercup.

Yellow flower and immature bur.

Seedling showing deeply toothed leaves.

Sulfur cinquefoil
Potentilla recta L.

Sulfur cinquefoil
Rosaceae
(Rose family)

Sulfur cinquefoil is a perennial, 1 to 1 1/2 feet tall, with well developed root-stocks. Leaves palmately compound with 5 or 7 toothed leaflets on each leaf. Leaves that are sparsely hairy appear green on the underside rather than silvery as in many *Potentilla* species. Flowers light yellow with 5 petals, each flower producing numerous single-seeded oval achenes.

Sulfur cinquefoil is often found in disturbed areas such as roadsides and pastures. Colonies of plants are also often seen in undisturbed sites. Flowering occurs from May to July.

Each compound leaf has from 5 to 7 toothed leaflets.

Light yellow flowers have 5 petals that are deeply notched. Yellow centers of flowers contain numerous stamens.

Catchweed bedstraw
Galium aparine L.

Catchweed bedstraw
Rubiaceae
(Madder family)

Native annual with slender taproots. The square stems have downward-pointing bristles, are weak, often tangling and may be up to 80 inches long. Leaves linear, stiff-hairy, mostly in whorls of 6 to 8. Flowers are minute, white, 4-parted, and borne on short branches in the leaf axils. Fruits are 2 nearly round halves, densely covered by fine hooked hairs.

Catchweed bedstraw is common throughout the region, and in recent years has become a serious weed in cultivated fields, particularly in hay or grain fields where it clings to, and tangles with the crop, making harvest difficult. The small bristly-hooked fruits also cling to wool, hair, and clothing. A related species, northern bedstraw (*G. boreale* L.), is perennial, reproducing by seed and creeping roots. This native differs from catchweed bedstraw by the creeping roots, the leaves are in whorls of 4, and the stem is erect.

Non-standard name: cleavers.

Catchweed bedstraw flowers, borne on short branches in leaf axils, develop into 2-parted fruit.

Cross section of catchweed bedstraw – note the square stem, leaves in a whorl, and back-pointing bristles on the leaves.

Lesser snapdragon
Antirrhinum orontium L.

Lesser snapdragon
Scrophulariaceae
(Figwort family)

Annual with stems that are much branched and 8 to 20 inches tall. The leaves are linear and 3/4 to 2 inches long. Flowers are axillary, pink-purple and about 5/8 inch long. The fruit is asymmetrical, opening by pores to release the numerous seeds.

Lesser snapdragon has been found in coastal regions of Oregon, Washington and California.

Flowers in the leaf axils near the plant tops.

Asymmetrical, hairy fruit capsule with persistent style.

Foxglove
Digitalis purpurea L.

Foxglove
Scrophulariaceae
(Figwort family)

A large biennial with erect stems usually 3 to 6 feet tall but has been reported up to 12 feet tall. The lower leaves are up to 1 or more feet long and 5 inches wide with leaf margins that are toothed. The upper leaves are progressively smaller. Flowers are 1 1/2 to 2 3/8 inches long, nodding, white to pink to reddish purple, the lower side paler and dark-spotted within. The fruits contain many minute seeds.

A native of Europe that is well established in the Pacific Coast states. Originally introduced as an ornamental and for medicinal purposes, it now occurs in logged areas, along roadsides and in coastal pastures. It is reported to be toxic to livestock.

Pink tubular flowers of foxglove.

Grouping of foxglove showing color variation in flowers.

Sharppoint fluvellin
Kickxia elatine (L.) Dumort.

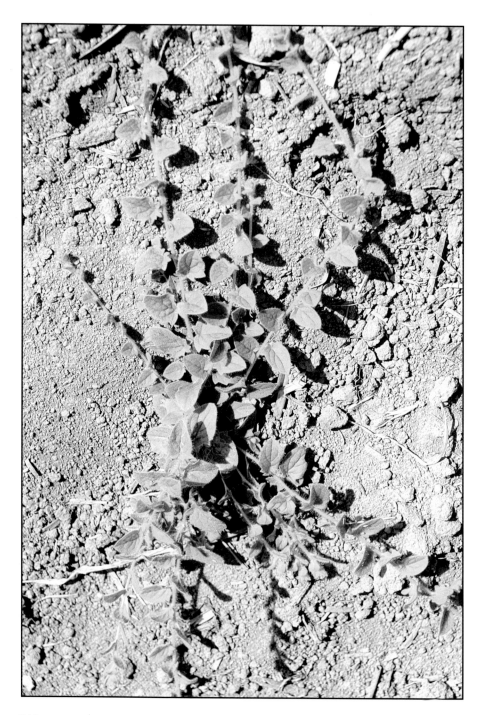

Sharppoint fluvellin
Scrophulariaceae
(Figwort family)

Creeping annual, much-branched, soft-hairy and somewhat sticky. The leaves are alternate, 1/2 to 1 inch long, early leaves are rounded but later leaves are usually broadly arrowhead-shaped but sometimes with more than one pair of basal lobes. Flowers are borne singly from the leaf axils on thread-like stalks up to 1 inch in length. Each is about 3/8 to 1/2 inch long including the spur. Flowers are 2-lipped, white to pale yellow with a purple upper lip. The fruit is nearly round, 3/16 inch across or less, opening at the top to release seeds.

Sharppoint fluvellin is native to Europe. It can be found growing in moist, sandy soil, and is beginning to occur as a problem in nursery stock and field crops. Female fluvellin (*K. spuria* (L.) Dumort.) is similar but with rounded leaves.

Non-standard names: cancerwort and fluvellin for sharppoint fluvellin; roundleaf fluvellin for female fluvellin.

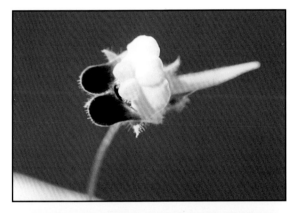

Irregular flowers have a spur.

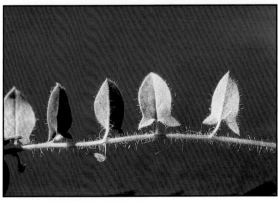

Early leaves of sharppoint fluvellin are rounded but later become broadly arrowhead-shaped.

Dalmatian toadflax
Linaria genistifolia ssp. *dalmatica* (L.) Maire and Petitmengin

Dalmatian toadflax
Scrophulariaceae
(Figwort family)

Dalmatian toadflax is a perennial, up to 3 feet tall, reproducing by seed and underground root stalks. Leaves are dense, alternate, entire, upper leaves are conspicuously broad-based. Flowers are borne in axils of upper leaves and are 2-lipped, 3/4 to 1 1/2 inches long with a long spur, yellow with an orange, bearded throat. Fruit a 2-celled capsule with many irregularly angled seeds.

Dalmatian toadflax was introduced from southeastern Europe, probably as an ornamental. It is aggressive and may be found along roadsides and on rangeland where it may become a serious problem by crowding out desirable forage. An extensive and deep root system along with a waxy leaf make this an extremely difficult plant to control.

Early spring growth of this prolific perennial has waxy leaves with a blue-green color. Leaves individually clasp the stem.

Yellow flowers with long spurs appear at mid-summer with plants continuing to flower until early fall.

547

Yellow toadflax
Linaria vulgaris Mill.

Yellow toadflax
Scrophulariaceae
(Figwort family)

Yellow toadflax is perennial, 1 to 2 feet tall, reproducing by seed and underground rootstocks. Leaves are pale green, numerous, narrow, pointed at both ends, 2 1/2 or more inches long. Flowers are 1 inch long with a bearded, orange throat. Fruit is round, 1/4 inch in diameter, brown, 2-celled, with many seeds. Seeds are dark brown to black, 1/12 inch in diameter, flattened with a papery circular wing.

Yellow toadflax is a native of Eurasia, introduced to the United States in the mid-1800s as an ornamental. This creeping perennial is an aggressive invader of rangelands, displacing desirable grasses. It is also found along roadsides, waste places, and cultivated fields. An extensive root system makes this plant difficult to control.

Non-standard name: butter and eggs.

Narrow leaves that are pointed at both ends are less than 2 1/2 inches long and are individually connected to the central stem.

Yellow flowers with an orange throat have spur-like appendages.

549

Moth mullein
Verbascum blattaria L.

Moth mullein
Scrophulariaceae
(Figwort family)

Taprooted biennial, producing a basal rosette of leaves in the first year which may persist through the second year, producing in the second year a single stem, 1 1/2 to 5 feet in height. Leaves of the rosette dark green, often reddish-tinged, usually shallowly lobed and toothed, tapering to a short stalk; leaves of the flowering stem merely toothed, becoming progressively reduced upwards, sessile and more or less clasping the stem. Flowers bright yellow or occasionally nearly white, 3/4 to 1 1/4 inches wide, slightly irregularly 5-lobed. Fruit splitting open to release the numerous seeds. Seeds widest at the top, grooved and deeply pitted.

Moth mullein is a native of Europe that is now widespread in the U.S. It flowers from May to September. It occurs along roadsides, in waste areas, pastures and, occasionally, in perennial crops.

Leaves are dark green, very shallowly lobed and toothed, tapering to a short stalk.

Flowers are bright yellow, 3/4 to 1 1/4 inches wide, 5-lobed with maroon colored centers.

551

Common mullein
Verbascum thapsus L.

Common mullein
Scrophulariaceae
(Figwort family)

This biennial produces a large, thick rosette of fuzzy leaves the first year and a single, stout, erect stem, 2 to 6 feet tall, the second year. The leaves are alternate, overlapping one another, light green, densely woolly. Flowers are sessile, borne in long terminal spikes, sulfur yellow, 5-lobed and more than an inch in diameter. Fruits are 2-chambered with numerous, small, angular, brownish seeds, 1/32 inch long.

This weed was introduced from Europe, but it is a native of Asia and is common throughout the temperate parts of North America. It is a common sight along river bottoms, in pastures, meadows, fence rows and waste areas, especially on gravelly soils. Because of the large number of seeds produced by each plant, it is difficult to control. Livestock will not eat the plant because of its woolliness. Flowering and seed production occur from June to August.

Common mullein produces a rosette the first year of its two-year life cycle. Leaves of this plant are covered with soft, fine hair.

Yellow 5-lobed flowers are borne in long spikes in late summer.

Bilobed speedwell
Veronica biloba L.

Bilobed speedwell
Scrophulariaceae
(Figwort family)

A shallow taprooted annual growing 2 to 12 inches tall. Stems may be single or branched, erect or spreading. Leaves are covered with short, stiff or glandular hairs, coarsely toothed, and normally less than 1 inch long. Flowers in terminal racemes of 1 to 25, blue and inconspicuous. Pale yellow seeds are contained in a flattened 2-lobed capsule that is cleft nearly to the base.

Capsule shape is perhaps the most reliable characteristic in distinguishing bilobed speedwell from other annual *Veronica* species. Bilobed speedwell was introduced from Asia. It is known as snow speedwell in some regions, and was listed as *V. campylopoda* Boiss. in some early publications. It is one of the first weeds to appear and complete its life cycle in the spring, taking advantage of early soil moisture, and thereby able to thrive in areas of limited precipitation. Bilobed speedwell is abundant in fields, foothills, waste places, and disturbed sites throughout many parts of the arid and semi-arid West, and a frequent problem in dryland wheat in the Great Basin region.

Flowers of bilobed speedwell are small, with blue petal margins and a white center.

Seedlings have heart-shaped cotyledons and toothed leaves.

Purslane speedwell
Veronica peregrina L.

Purslane speedwell
Scrophulariaceae
(Figwort family)

An annual with stems that are usually much branched, erect or somewhat spreading, up to 12 inches tall. The leaves are linear, alternate or paired in the lower part of the plant. Lower leaves are short-petioled, upper leaves sessile. The flowers are minute, white and borne in leaf axils. The fruit is heart-shaped.

This species is native to the U.S. There are varieties that are glandular-hairy and others that are smooth.

Minute white flowers are borne in leaf axils.

The fruit of purslane speedwell is heart-shaped.

Persian speedwell
Veronica persica Poir.

Persian speedwell
Scrophulariaceae
(Figwort family)

Annual or winter annual that forms a dense groundcover. Stems are weak, prostrate, often with ascending tips. Lower leaves are paired on the stem, while the upper leaves are alternate. Leaf blades are somewhat longer than broad, coarsely toothed, with short petioles. Flowers are sky-blue having dark stripes with white centers and are borne on long slender stalks in the leaf axils. Fruits are heart-shaped and hairy.

A native of Eurasia, this plant was probably introduced as a border or rock garden ornamental. It is now widespread in the United States.

Non-standard names: birdseye speedwell and winter speedwell.

Persian speedwell has a heart-shaped fruit which develops from an irregular flower.

Notice the 3-lobed margin of ivyleaf speedwell (V. hederifolia L.) (left) compared to the toothed leaf-margin of Persian speedwell (right).

Sacred datura
Datura innoxia Mill.

Sacred datura
Solanaceae
(Nightshade family)

Sacred datura is a large, conspicuous grayish-green perennial with stems up to 3 feet tall and covered with fine gray hairs, giving the plant a waxy appearance. Leaves are alternate, egg-shaped, with petioles 1 to 5 inches long. Leaf blades green on the upper surface and grayish underneath, 3 to 10 inches long, remotely and inconspicuously toothed, and have conspicuous whitish veins. Flowers are white or pale lavender, broadly funnel-shaped, 6 to 10 inches across, with 5 slender teeth that are 1/2 to 3/4 inch long. The seedpod is covered with spines which are less than 3/8 inch long. Seeds are light yellowish-brown.

Sacred datura is a native perennial that grows in dry, sandy and gravelly soils. Small datura (*D. discolor* Bernh.) is a related annual plant which forms large clumps. Flowers of this plant are white, tinged with violet, mostly 2 to 4 inches long, 2 inches or less wide and have 10 slender teeth on the flower. Small datura is toxic and the sacred datura is hallucinogenic.

Non-standard name of small datura: desert thornapple.

The trumpet-shaped, white to lavender flowers of sacred datura have a 5-toothed corolla.

Globe-shaped seedpods of sacred datura contain many seeds.

Jimsonweed
Datura stramonium L.

Jimsonweed
Solanaceae
(Nightshade family)

A rank-smelling annual with stems 3/4 to 5 feet tall. Leaves alternate, large, usually unevenly toothed to shallowly lobed. Flowers trumpet-shaped, 3 1/2 to 5 inches long, white in *D. stramonium* var. *stramonium* and purplish in *D. stramonium* var. *tatula* (L.) Torr. Fruits about 2 inches long, fleshy at first, but becoming dry and hard, covered by stout prickles. Seeds numerous, flattened, dark brown to black, minutely pitted.

Jimsonweed, thought to be of North American origin, is found on dry rangelands, vacant lots, and waste places. It is a source of hyoscyamine, a drug used as a sedative and hypnotic. The entire plant is toxic and people have been poisoned by seeds, flowers and leaves. Flowering occurs June to September.

Non-standard names: Jamestown weed, thornapple.

The prickly fruit is located in the axils of stems and contains numerous seeds.

Flowers are trumpet-shaped, 3 1/2 to 5 inches long. Colors range from white to purplish.

Black henbane
Hyoscyamus niger L.

Black henbane
Solanaceae
(Nightshade family)

Black henbane may be annual or biennial, 1 to 3 feet tall. Leaves are coarsely-toothed to shallowly lobed and pubescent. Foliage has a foul odor. Flowers, on long racemes in axils of upper leaves, are brownish-yellow with a purple center and purple veins. Fruits are approximately 1 inch long, 5-lobed.

Black henbane is a native of Europe and has been cultivated as an ornamental. It has spread throughout the United States and is a common weed of pastures, fencerows, roadsides, and waste areas. Black henbane contains hyoscyamine and other alkaloids which have caused occasional livestock poisoning. However, the plant is usually not grazed by animals and is consumed only when more palatable forage is not available. Henbane alkaloids have been used in the past , and are currently used, as medicines at controlled dosages. It is considered a poisonous plant to humans.

Large rosettes having serrated leaves covered with fine hair. The plant has a pungent odor at all growth stages.

Two rows of pineapple-shaped fruit, about 1 inch long, appear in early fall. Within each capsule are hundreds of tiny black seeds.

565

Virginia groundcherry
Physalis virginiana Mill.

Virginia groundcherry
Solanaceae
(Nightshade family)

This perennial is 12 to 30 inches tall, reproducing by seeds and rootstalks. Stems are hairy, erect, widely branching. Leaves are alternate, oval, 2 to 3 inches long, with wavy to bluntly-toothed margins. Flowers are bell-shaped, yellow, with dark centers. Fruit is round, 3/8 to 1/2 inch in diameter, fleshy, with many seeds. Seeds are 1/20 inch in diameter, yellow, oval, flattened.

Virginia groundcherry is a native plant in the same family as potatoes and tomatoes. It grows in cultivated fields, along roadsides, ditches and in waste areas. It is especially troublesome in bean fields. Control of this perennial is difficult. Identification is difficult because of the similarity of species.

Immature plants of Virginia groundcherry have narrow leaves, 2 to 3 inches long, with bluntly toothed margins.

Bell-shaped, yellow flowers with dark centers develop into a bladder-like, pear-shaped case which encloses the seed-bearing fruit.

Wright groundcherry
Physalis wrightii Gray

Wright groundcherry
Solanaceae
(Nightshade family)

Summer annual with a bushy growth habit from 1 to 5 feet in height with alternate leaves which vary from 2 to 5 inches in length and 1/4 to 2 inches in width. Leaves are oblong or egg-shaped and mostly pointed at the tip. Leaf margins are irregularly toothed or cut and sometimes wavy. Flowers are wheel-shaped, whitish, 1/2 to 3/4 inch wide, with a large yellow stigma and purplish anthers. The fruit is borne on a thread-like stalk that bends down under the weight of the fruit. Calyx is papery and encloses the fruit, looking like a green Chinese lantern.

Lanceleaf groundcherry (*P. lanceifolia* Nees) is similar to Wright ground-cherry but leaves are entire to slightly toothed and the flowers are more yellow. Both lanceleaf groundcherry and Wright groundcherry are found in the Southwest from Texas to California in cultivated fields and disturbed waste areas. They flower from April to November.

The inflated, papery calyx encloses the fruit, forming a miniature "Chinese lantern."

The seedling plant of Wright groundcherry has lance-shaped leaves with irregular margins.

569

Bittersweet nightshade
Solanum dulcamara L.

Bittersweet nightshade
Solanaceae
(Nightshade family)

A trailing or climbing perennial with spreading stems up to 10 feet. Leaves dark green to sometimes dark purplish, 1 to 4 inches long, often with one to several lobes or leaflets at the base. Flowers are star-shaped, having purple petals and prominent yellow or orange anthers. Fruits are bright red, egg-shaped berries, arranged in open clusters.

Bittersweet nightshade is a native of Europe that is widely distributed throughout much of North America. It is typically found growing in moist waste areas, in fence rows, along drainage ditches and waterways; and may form large colonies or thickets. It also becomes established in orchards, vineyards, and residential landscapes. All parts of the plant are toxic. Children seem to be especially attracted to the bright red berries, which may cause poisoning if eaten in sufficient quantity.

Non-standard name: bitter nightshade.

Flowers are star-shaped with purple petals and bright yellow anthers. Fruits turn from green, to yellow, to bright red as berries mature.

Dark green leaves are heart-shaped, often having basal lobes or leaflets.

571

Silverleaf nightshade
Solanum elaeagnifolium Cav.

Silverleaf nightshade
Solanaceae
(Nightshade family)

A perennial, 1 to 3 feet tall, spreading by rhizomes or seeds. Stems are sparsely covered with short yellow thorns. Leaves and stems are covered with dense short hairs that give the foliage a gray or silvery appearance. Leaves are narrow, lance-shaped, with entire to wavy margins. Flowers are 3/4 to 1 inch wide with violet to light blue (sometimes white) petals. The mature fruit is a yellow or dull orange berry, which may eventually turn blackish.

Silverleaf nightshade is native to the central United States, but has spread to other areas where it is found on rangeland, in pastures, waste areas, and cropland. The berries and foliage are poisonous to livestock. This plant should not be confused with the true horsenettle *(S. carolinense* L.), which is also a rhizomatous perennial, but lacks a dense silvery covering of hairs and has broader, more toothed leaves, and more prominent spines.

Non-standard name: white horsenettle.

Stems are covered with scruffy, short hairs and have yellow thorns.

Flowers of silverleaf nightshade are blue to violet and have 5 petals with yellow anthers in the center. Fruit are yellow or orange and are filled with seed.

573

Black nightshade
Solanum nigrum L.

Black nightshade
Solanaceae
(Nightshade family)

An annual 6 to 24 inches tall with glabrous or appressed-hairy stems. Leaves are ovate, smooth to wavy-edged and tapered to the tip. Flowers resemble those of the potato and tomato and are white to pale-blue, 1/4 to 3/8 inch wide, borne in clusters. Calyx is scarcely enlarging, not cupping the fruit.

Black nightshade, a native of Europe, is a weed of waste places and cultivated fields. The berries frequently become mixed with harvested commodities such as dry beans and green peas, decreasing crop quality. The green (immature) fruit and foliage contain toxic alkaloids. In recent years, nightshades have become troublesome in fields where certain herbicides have been used to control other weeds but are weak on nightshade.

Eastern black nightshade (*S. ptycanthum* Dun.) is not normally found in our area.

Non-standard name: garden nightshade.

Black nightshade seedling leaves are ovate and taper to a pointed tip.

Fruits of black nightshade are black when mature. The calyx, or covering on the top of the berry, is smaller than on hairy nightshade (S. Sarrachoides Sendtner). Stems and leaves have a smooth appearance.

575

Buffalobur
Solanum rostratum Dun.

Buffalobur
Solanaceae
(Nightshade family)

This native annual grows to 2 feet high, has leaves 2 to 5 inches long with deep lobes and is covered with spines. Yellow, 5-lobed flowers, common throughout the summer, are about 1 inch wide. The berry is enclosed by an enlarged calyx and contains many seeds. Seeds are black, wrinkled and flattened.

Buffalobur is widely distributed in the western U.S. It is common on disturbed wastelands and prairies. It is most common on sandy soils, but grows on most soils. It is drought resistant and serves as a host for the Colorado potato beetle. It is not a highly competitive species and can be controlled with herbicides.

Leaves of seedling plants of buffalobur are deeply lobed and spiny on the underside with prominent veins.

Yellow flowers appear in early summer and develop into a spiny seed capsule containing many small seeds.

Hairy nightshade
Solanum sarrachoides Sendtner

Hairy Nightshade
Solanaceae
(Nightshade family)

Hairy nightshade is an annual, 12 to 24 inches tall. Foliage is spreading, hairy, and may feel sticky when handled. Flowers resemble those of potato and tomato and have 5 white petals, and an enlarging green calyx. They are arranged in clusters. As the fruit matures, the calyx cups the lower half of the greenish or yellowish fruit.

Hairy nightshade, a native of South America, is a widespread weed of waste places and cultivated fields. The plant contains toxic alkaloids, especially in the berries. Hairy nightshade causes problems in field crops similar to those described for black nightshade.

Plants start their growth in early summer. Leaves and stems are quite hairy.

White flowers, having 5 petals with yellow centers, develop into green fruit containing very small seeds. Each berry is half-enclosed by the calyx.

Turkeyberry
Solanum torvum Swartz

Turkeyberry
Solanaceae
(Nightshade family)

Turkeyberry is a perennial, up to 10 feet tall, with hooked prickles on the stems and leaves. Leaves are simple, alternate, ovate, lobed, and up to 7 inches in length. Flowers are white, about 1 inch in diameter, with prominent yellow stamens and in clusters. Fruits are yellow-green when mature, 1/2 inch in diameter, and numerous-seeded.

Turkeyberry was introduced, probably from Asia. It forms dense, thorny stands in pastures, forests, and waste areas. It is present in Hawaii on the islands of Oahu, Maui, and Hawaii. It has a great potential to spread since fruits are produced throughout the year, and seeds can number between 300 to 400 per fruit. The fruits are apparently used in Southeast Asian cooking.

Fruits, about 1/2 inch in diameter, contain many seeds.

Seedlings of turkeyberry resemble those of cultivated eggplants.

581

Cutleaf nightshade
Solanum triflorum Nutt.

Cutleaf nightshade
Solanaceae
(Nightshade family)

This plant is an annual, 4 to 24 inches tall, branched from the base, with ill-smelling foliage. Leaves are deeply lobed and may have short pubescence. Flowers resemble those of potato and tomato and are small, have white petals and a somewhat enlarging calyx and are arranged in groups of three. Fruits are green.

Cutleaf nightshade is native to North America east of the Cascade Mountains to the Great Plains and is a weed of waste places and cultivated fields. The plant contains toxic alkaloids. Cutleaf nightshade is resistant to many commonly used herbicides.

Seedlings of cutleaf nightshade have deeply lobed leaves and are covered with short hair. Seedlings commonly appear in early spring.

Flowers of cutleaf nightshade are white with 5 petals and yellow stamens in the center. Fruit are abundant and contain many yellow seeds.

583

Saltcedar
Tamarix ramosissima Ledeb.

Saltcedar
Tamaricaceae
(Tamarisk family)

Deciduous or evergreen shrubs or small trees, 5 to 20 feet tall. Bark on saplings and stems is reddish-brown. Leaves are small and scale-like, on highly-branched slender stems. Flowers are pink to white, 5-petalled.

Saltcedar, also called tamarisk, was introduced from Eurasia and is now widespread in the United States. Smallflower tamarisk (*T. parviflora* DC.) is similar in appearance, but has 4-petalled flowers, with brown to deep purple bark on stems. Smallflower tamarisk was introduced from southern Europe, and is also widespread. Both species are used as ornamentals, but have escaped and become naturalized along streams, canals, and reservoirs in much of the West.

Flowers are pink, small, 5-petalled, and borne in finger-like clusters. Leaves are scale-like, on slender, highly-branched, green stems.

Smooth woody stems are dark brown to reddish-brown.

Common cattail
Typha latifolia L.

Common cattail
Typhaceae
(Cattail family)

Tall perennial herbs with large creeping rhizomes. Stems are simple, cylindrical, erect and pithy. Leaves are long, linear, broad, flat, parallel-veined, and rather spongy. Mature inflorescences are velvety-brown, densely crowded, terminal, spike-like, cylindrical heads. These eventually fall apart, releasing clouds of tiny tufted, air-borne fruits.

Cattail is commonly found in wet or marshy places throughout the West, where it provides habitat for waterfowl and other wildlife. Though cattail is not generally considered a weed, its presence in water storage ponds or along irrigation canals and ditches can reduce holding capacity or impede waterflow.

Large creeping rhizomes readily propagate new shoots, allowing dense stands to develop.

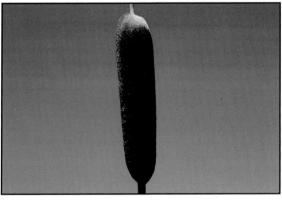

Velvety-brown seedheads break apart, releasing many air-borne fruits.

Stinging nettle
Urtica dioica L.

Stinging nettle
Urticaceae
(Nettle family)

A perennial slow-spreading plant, with 4-angled stems, 2 to 9 feet tall. Leaves coarsely-toothed, opposite, with numerous, small, bristly, stinging hairs over much of their surface. Greenish flower clusters are of two types, with staminate and pistillate flowers usually on different plants. Clusters are borne on slender branches in axils of upper leaves.

Stinging nettle is a native species, confined primarily to shaded, moist areas along streams, or in deep, rich, undisturbed soils. It is primarily a nuisance to recreationists because of its stinging hairs. It also produces impenetrable, unmanageable stands along waterways used for livestock or irrigation purposes.

Leaves of stinging nettle are coarsely-toothed, forming opposite pairs. Stems are square. Undersides of leaves and stems have small needle-like structures.

Green flower clusters are attached to the axil of the leaf and stem.

589

Prostrate vervain
Verbena bracteata Lag. & Rodr.

Prostrate vervain
Verbenaceae
(Verbena family)

A rough-hairy annual, or more often perennial, prostrate weed with diffuse branches 1/2 to 1 1/2 feet long. Leaves are 3-parted or 3-lobed. Flowers are pinkish to pale blue, borne in long dense spikes, with long leaf-like bracts extending well beyond the flowers. Fruits are gray to brown, under 1/16 inch long and are ridged and roughened.

Prostrate vervain is widely distributed in North America, where it typically infests fields, roadsides, waste areas, and other disturbed sites.

Small trumpet-shaped flowers are borne in long spikes, with a green bract extending beyond each flower.

Vervain seedlings have leaves that are deeply lobed and toothed.

591

Blue vervain
Verbena hastata L.

Blue vervain
Verbenaceae
(Verbena family)

An erect perennial 3 to 5 feet tall, spread by seed and by short rhizomes. Stems and foliage are roughly hairy. Leaves opposite or whorled, lance-shaped, with serrate or toothed margins. Flowers blue to purplish or pink in straight spikes which are arranged in upright panicles.

Prostrate vervain (*V. bracteata* Lag. and Rodr.) also has blue flowers arranged in spikes, but is a spreading or prostrate annual, or more often perennial, with 3-parted or 3-lobed leaves, and elongated leaf-like bracts. Blue vervain is found in wet meadows, marshes, and riparian habitats throughout the United States and Canada. Prostrate vervain can be a weed of pastures, grain fields, lawns, roadsides, and waste areas.

Flowers open as progressive single rings on vertical spike-like inflorescences.

Opposite or whorled lance-shaped leaves of blue vervain have serrated margins.

593

Field violet
Viola arvensis Murr.

Field violet
Violaceae
(Violet family)

An annual with stems erect, to prostrate and branched. Leaves are ovate to lanceolate and coarsely toothed and about the same length as the petioles. Stipules are large and divided into 5 to 9 segments, the terminal segment often nearly as large as the main blade. The flowers are whitish or light yellow and showy.

A European plant that has escaped from cultivation to become an occasional problem.

Non-standard name: wild pansy.

Field violet flowers are typical pansy flowers and are white to light yellow.

Ovate leaves of field violet have coarsely toothed margins.

Creosotebush
Larrea tridentata (Sesse & Moc. ex DC.) Coville

Creosotebush
Zygophyllaceae
(Caltrop family)

Creosotebush is a much branched, strong-scented, resinous evergreen shrub, up to 12 feet tall. Leaves are opposite, with 2 widely divergent, sessile, asymmetrical olive-green leaflets that are oblong to broader at the tip than at the base, and united at the base. Flowers are axillary, solitary, and have 5 yellow, clawed petals. The fruiting structure is a rounded, villose, 5-celled capsule that separates at maturity into 5 indehiscent 1-seeded carpels.

Creosotebush is a dominant shrub over great areas of desert, on dry slopes, and plains, and has been reported to be of economical value because of its antiseptic properties and medicinal uses.

This evergreen plant has a characteristic odor associated with its resinous leaves.

Flowers found in the leaf axils are yellow and give rise to a 5-celled capsule.

African rue
Peganum harmala L.

African rue
Zygophyllaceae
(Caltrop family)

A much-branched perennial herb. Leaves are alternate, smooth, and finely and deeply cut or divided with long, narrow segments. Flowers have 5 white petals. The fruit is a 2- to 4-celled, many-seeded capsule.

African rue is a native of north African and Asiatic deserts. The first report in North America occurred in 1928 near Deming, New Mexico. It has since spread across New Mexico and is reported in Arizona, Texas, Washington and Oregon. It has been reported to be toxic to domestic ruminants in experimental feeding studies. The seeds are more toxic than the leaves.

Leaves are finely divided in long segments and the flower has 5 white petals.

The fruit of African rue is a 2- to 4-celled capsule.

599

Puncturevine
Tribulus terrestris L.

Puncturevine
Zygophyllaceae
(Caltrop family)

Puncturevine is annual, prostrate or somewhat ascending, mat forming, with trailing stems, each 1/2 to 5 feet long. Leaves opposite, hairy, divided into 4 to 8 pairs of leaflets, each about 1/4 to 1/2 inch long and oval. Flowers are yellow, 1/3 to 1/2 inch wide with 5 petals, borne in the leaf axils. Fruits consist of 5 sections which, at maturity, break into tack-like structures with sharp, sometimes curving spines, each section 2- to 4-seeded.

Puncturevine was introduced from southern Europe and is now widely scattered over much of the U.S. It grows in pastures, cultivated fields, waste areas, and along highways and roads. The hard, spiny burs damage wool, are undesirable in hay, and may be injurious to livestock. Bicycle tires are frequently punctured by the burs. The seed will remain dormant in the soil for 4 to 5 years, which makes eradication difficult. Because of its sharp burs, puncturevine has been spread over a wide area by animals and vehicles. Flowering and seed production occur from July to October.

Non-standard names: goathead, Mexican sandbur, Texas sandbur.

Seedling puncturevine leaves are pinnately compound with hairs appearing on each leaflet.

Puncturevine flowers, yellow with 5 petals, develop into circular spiny fruit that break into sections when ripe.

601

Glossary

Accrescent – Enlarging with age.

Achene – A small dry, one-seeded fruit which does not split at maturity.

Acute – Ending in a sharp point.

Adventitious – In an unusual or unexpected place.

Aerial – In the air.

Allelopathic substances – Chemical compounds produced by plants that affect the interactions between different plants, including microorganisms.

Alternate – Singly along a stem; one leaf or bud at node.

Anthesis – Flowering; when pollination takes place.

Apex – The tip.

Appressed – Pressed flatly against the surface.

Ascending – Growing upward in an upturned position.

Auricle – Having small ear-shaped lobe or appendage.

Awn – A slender, usually terminal bristle.

Axil – The angle between a leaf and stem.

Axillary – Between the petiole or branch and the stem.

Biennial – A plant which lives two years.

Bract – A small leaf-like structure below a flower.

Calyx – The outer parts of a flower composed of usually leaf-like parts called sepals.

Capillary – Hairlike, slender and thread-like.

Caudex – The main stem of a plant at or just below the ground surface.

Chlorophyll – The green coloring matter of plants.

Clasping – Blade of the leaf extending beyond and surrounding the stem.

Clavate – Club-shaped.

Conical – Cone-shaped.

Cordate – Heart-shaped.

Corolla – The petals of a flower surrounding the stamens and pistil.

Crenate – With rounded teeth; scalloped.

Cylindrical – Having the form or shape of a cylinder.

Cyme – A short and broad, somewhat flat-topped flower cluster in which the central flower blooms first.

Deciduous – Leaves falling at maturity or the end of a growing season.

Decompound – Divided into compound divisions; repeatedly compound.

Decumbent – Lying on the ground at the base, but rising at the tip.

Depauperate - Stunted.

Dimorphic – Occurring in two distinct forms.

Disk flower – A tubular flower in members of the sunflower family.

Elliptic – Oval or oblong with rounded ends and more than twice as long as broad.

Entire – Leaf margins that are not cut or toothed.

Filament – Anther-bearing stalk of a stamen; thread.

Floret – One of the closely clustered small flowers that make up the flower head of a composite flower. Grass flower consisting of a lemma, palea, stamens and/or pistil.

Frond – The leaf of a fern.

Glabrous – Smooth; without hairs.

Glume – Bract at the base of a grass spikelet.

Indehiscent – Not opening at maturity.

Inflorescence – The flowering part of the plant.

Involucre – A circle of bracts under a flower cluster.

Keel – A ridge; the two united front petals of a flower.

Lanceolate – Lance-shaped.

Leaflet – One small blade of a compound leaf.

Ligule – A thin, membranous outgrowth or fringe of hairs from the base of the blade of most grasses.

Linear – Long and narrow with parallel sides.

Lobed – Cut into shallow segments.

Membranous – Thin and transparent.

Midrib – Central vein of a leaf.

Multifloreted – Many flowered.

Obicular – Circular.

Oblanceolate – Lance-shaped, tapering at both ends with the broadest part at tip end.

Obovoid – Egg-shaped with broader part at top.

Opposite –Arranged on the same node at the opposite side of the stem.

Orbicular – Circular.

Ovary – The seed-bearing part of the pistil.

Ovate – Egg-shaped with broader part at base.

Palmate – Spreading like the fingers from the palm.

Panicle – Loose, irregularly compound flowering part of plant with flowers borne on individual stalks.

Pappus – Bristles, scales, awns or short crown at tip of achene in flowers of sunflower family.

Pedicel – Stalk of a single flower.

Peduncle – Stalk of a flower cluster or individual solitary flower.

Perennial – A plant living more than two years.

Perfect flower – Having both stamens and pistils in the same flower.

Petiole – Stem or stalk of a leaf.

Phloem – The food-transporting tissue of a plant.

Pinnate – Arising from several different points along the sides of an axis.

Pinnatifid – Pinnately cleft.

Pistillate – Bearing pistils but no stamens.

Prostrate – Lying against the ground.

Pubescent – Covered with hairs.

Raceme – Arrangement of flowers along a stem on individual stalks about equal in length.

Rachis – The main stem bearing flowers or leaves.

Ray flower – Marginal petal-like flowers of some composites.

Receptacle – The part of the stem to which the flower is attached.

Reflexed – Turned abruptly downward or backward.

Reticulate – Net-like.

Rhizomatous – Having rhizomes.

Rhizome – Underground stem, usually lateral, sending out shoots above ground and roots below.

Rosette – Compact cluster of leaves arranged in an often basal circle.

Rugose – Wrinkled.

Scale – Thin, dry membrane, usually foliar.

Sepal – One division of the calyx.

Serrate – Saw-toothed, with sharp, forward-pointing teeth.

Sessile – Without a stalk.

Sheath – Lower part of the leaf which surrounds the stem.

Silicle – A short silique, almost equally as long as wide.

Silique – Elongated capsule with a septum separating in two valves.

Simple leaves – Unbranched, not compound.

Spatulate – Spoon-shaped, narrow at base and wide at apex.

Spike – A usually long inflorescence with sessile flowers.

Spikelet – Small or secondary spike; flower cluster in grasses consisting of usually 2 glumes, and one or more florets.

Spinose – Full of spines.

Stamen – The pollen-bearing organ of a flowering plant.

Staminate – Having stamens but no pistils.

Stellate – Star-shaped.

Stigma – Part of the pistil that receives the pollen.

Stolon – A horizontal stem which roots at the nodes.

Striate – Marked with parallel lines or ridges.

Subtended – Underneath, directly below and close to.

Succulent – Fleshy.

Terete – Circular in cross section.

Toothed – Sawteeth-like projections on the margins of the blade.

Tuberous – Like a tuber or producing tubers.

Tufted – In compact clusters.

Umbel – A flat or rounded flower cluster in which the stalks radiate from the same point, like the ribs of an umbrella.

Utricle – Small, inflated, 1-seeded, usually indehiscent fruit.

Veins – Ribs of a leaf; vascular bundles of a leaf.

Wing – A thin, membranous extension of a leaf blade.

Key to the Families of Weeds of the West

Nonflowering Plants

Flowering Plants (Remainder of the Key)

Monocot Key

10(9)   Plants with woody stems; leaves thick and fibrous
....AGAVE FAMILY (Agavaceae), pg. 2
Plants with herbaceous stems; leaves thin and nonfibrous
.... LILY FAMILY (Liliaceae), pg. 372

Dicot Key

11(3)   Corolla not present 13
Corolla present 12

12(11)   Petals distinct 22
Petals united, at least below 43

Dicots without Petals

13(11)   Calyx present, often petal-like 14
Calyx and corolla both absent; pistil one; flowers imperfect with
     pistillate and staminate flowers on same plant, borne in a
     cup-like structure; sap milky
     .... *Euphorbia* in SPURGE FAMILY (Euphorbiaceae), pg. 310

14(13)   Ovary superior; herbs or occasionally small bushy shrubs 15
Ovary inferior; woody shrubs
     ....OLEASTER FAMILY (Elaeagnaceae), pg. 304

15(14)   Ovary 3- to 5-celled .... *Ricinus* in SPURGE FAMILY
     (Euphorbiaceae), pg. 318
Ovary 1-celled 16

16(15)   Fruit a capsule, splitting at maturity; leaves opposite
     ....PINK FAMILY (Caryophyllaceae), pg. 250
Fruit dry, not splitting at maturity 17

17(16)   Stigma and style 1; herbage with stinging hairs
     ....NETTLE FAMILY (Urticaceae), pg. 588
Stigmas and styles 2 or several; herbage without stinging hairs 18

18(17)   Leaves with sheathing stipules
     .... BUCKWHEAT FAMILY (Polygonaceae), pg. 502
Leaves without sheathing stipules 19

19(18)   Stipules conspicuous, leafy; leaves palmately compound
     ....HEMP FAMILY (Cannabaceae), pg. 246
Stipules papery or none; leaves simple, pinnately veined 20

20(19)   Plants with scurfy leaves.................................... GOOSEFOOT FAMILY
     (Chenopodiaceae), pg. 268
Plants without scurfy leaves 21

21(20) Fruit triangular or a lens-like achene; stamens 4 to 9
............................BUCKWHEAT FAMILY (Polygonaceae), pg. 502
Fruit an urticle; stamens 3 to 5
............................AMARANTH FAMILY (Amaranthaceae), pg. 4

Dicots with Distinct Petals

22(12) Ovary superior (free from calyx) 23
Ovary inferior (more or less attached to the calyx) 41

23(22) Stamens attached to receptacle 24
Stamens attached to calyx or on a disk 38

24(23) Flowers with more than 10 stamens 25
Flowers with 10 or less stamens 29

25(24) Pistils 2 to many ......BUTTERCUP FAMILY (Ranunculaceae), pg. 524
Pistil 1 26

26(25) Leaves opposite ....ST. JOHNSWORT FAMILY (Clusiaceae), pg. 280
Leaves alternate or whorled 27

27(26) Ovary 5- to 30-celled; stamens numerous and united to form a tube
around the pistil ....MALLOW FAMILY (Malvaceae), pg. 382
Ovary 1-celled; stamens few, or if numerous, not united to form
a tube 28

28(27) Sepals falling off early; petals 4 or 6
....POPPY FAMILY (Papaveraceae), pg. 400
Sepals persistent; petals 5
.........*Calandrina* of PURSLANE FAMILY (Portulacaceae), pg. 518

29(24) Pistils more than 1 30
Pistil 1; styles or stigmas 1 or more 31

30(29) Pistils distinct, 3 to numerous
............................BUTTERCUP FAMILY (Ranunculaceae), pg. 524
Pistils more or less united around a central axis, 5 in number
....................................GERANIUM FAMILY (Geraniaceae) pg. 352

31(29) Flowers irregular 32
Flowers regular 33

32(31) Stamens 10, united in 1 or 2 sets; flowers usually in spikes, racemes
or heads ....PEA FAMILY (Fabaceae), pg. 320
Stamens 5; flowers usually solitary ....VIOLET FAMILY
(Violaceae) pg. 594

Dicots with United Petals

610

45(44)   Leaves compound ....WOODSORREL FAMILY
       (Oxalidaceae), pg. 398
      Leaves simple (may be palmately lobed)
       ....MALLOW FAMILY (Malvaceae), pg. 382

46(43)   Ovary superior (free from calyx) 47
      Ovary inferior (adherent to calyx) 55

47(46)   Corolla regular..48
      Corolla irregular or strongly 2-lipped 53

48(47)   Pistil 1 49
      Pistils 2 52

49(48)   Corolla dry and papery ....PLANTAIN FAMILY
       (Plantaginaceae), pg. 402
      Corolla colored, not dry and papery 50

50(49)   Ovary 4-celled, commonly 4-lobed; fruit of 4 nutlets; flower
       arrangement coiled ....BORAGE FAMILY
       (Boraginaceae), pg. 198
      Ovary 1-, 2-, or 3-celled; fruit a capsule or berry 51

51(50)   Calyx of 5 distinct sepals; fruit a capsule; plants climbing or trailing
       .................MORNINGGLORY FAMILY (Convolvulaceae), pg. 282
      Calyx 4 or 5 toothed or cleft; fruit a capsule or a berry; plants erect
       or diffuse ....NIGHTSHADE FAMILY (Solanaceae), pg. 560

52(48)   Stamens and stigmas united
       ....MILKWEED FAMILY (Asclepiadaceae), pg. 32
      Stamens and stigmas not united
       ....DOGBANE FAMILY (Apocynaceae), pg. 28

53(47)   Fruit a capsule; ovary 2-celled; stems usually round
       ....FIGWORT FAMILY (Scrophulariaceae), pg. 540
      Fruit of 2 to 4 nutlets; stems often square 54

54(53)   Fruit with 4 distinct nutlets; filaments much longer than anthers
       ....MINT FAMILY (Lamiaceae), pg. 362
      Fruit of 4 more or less fused nutlets; filaments about as long as
       anthers or shorter ....VERVAIN FAMILY
       (Verbenaceae), pg. 590

55(46)   Stamens distinct 56
      Stamens united into a tube around the style 58

56(55)	Ovary 1-celled; flowers in dense heads
.... TEASEL FAMILY (Dipsacaceae), pg. 302
Ovary more than 1-celled; flowers solitary, in racemes or open
inflorescences 57

57(56)	Ovary 2-celled; inflorescence mostly open
.... MADDER FAMILY (Rubiaceae), pg. 538
Ovary 2- to 5-celled; flowers solitary or in racemes, with a charac-
teristic bell shape .... BLUEBELL FAMILY
(Campanulaceae), pg. 244

58(55)	Flowers not in heads; vines with tendrils
.... CUCUMBER FAMILY (Cucurbitaceae), pg. 294
Flowers in heads; not vines or tendril bearing
.... SUNFLOWER FAMILY (Asteraceae), pg. 42

References

Alley, H.P. and G.A. Lee. 1979. *Weeds of Wyoming.* University of Wyoming Agricultural Experiment Station Bulletin 498, Laramie. 120 pp.

Dennis, L.J. 1980. *Gilkey's Weeds of the Pacific Northwest.* Oregon State University Press, Corvallis. 382 pp.

Dorn, R.D. 1977. *Manual of the Vascular Plants of Wyoming.* 2 vols. Garland Publishing, New York. 1498 pp.

Dorn, R.D. 1988. *Vascular Plants of Wyoming.* Mountain West Publishing, Cheyenne. 340 pp.

Gilkey, H.M. and L.J. Dennis. 1980. *Handbook of Northwestern Plants.* Oregon State University Press, Corvallis. 507 pp.

Goodrich, S. et al. 1986. *Uintah Basin Flora.* USDA Forest Service. 320 pp.

Great Plains Flora Association. 1986. *Flora of the Great Plains.* University Press of Kansas, Lawrence. 1392 pp.

Hawkes, R.B., L. Burrill, and L.J. Dennis. 1989. *A Guide to Selected Weeds of Oregon (Supplement).* Oregon Department of Agriculture, Salem. 50 pp.

Hawkes, R.B., T.D. Whitson, and L.J. Dennis. 1985. *A Guide to Selected Weeds of Oregon.* Oregon Department of Agriculture, Salem. 100 pp.

Hitchcock, C.L. and A. Cronquist. 1973. *Flora of the Pacific Northwest.* University of Washington Press, Seattle. 730 pp.

Hitchcock, C.L., A. Cronquist, M. Owenby, and J.W. Thompson. 1969. *Vascular Plants of the Pacific Northwest.* Vols. 1-5. University of Washington Press, Seattle. 2978 pp.

Holmgren, A.H. and B.A. Anderson. 1970. *Weeds of Utah.* Utah State University Agricultural Experiment Station Special Report 21, Logan. 115 pp.

James, L.F. et al. 1980. *Plants Poisonous to Livestock in the Western States.* USDA Agricultural Information Bulletin 415. 90 pp.

Johnson, J.R. and J.T. Nichols. 1982. *Plants of South Dakota Grasslands – A Photographic Study.* SDSU Agricultural Experiment Station Bulletin 566, Brookings. 166 pp.

Munz, P.A. and D.D. Keck. 1973. *A California Flora and Supplement.* University of California Press, Berkeley. 1681 (224) pp.

Nelson, E.W. and O. Burnside. 1979. *Nebraska Weeds.* Nebraska Department of Agriculture, Lincoln. 312 pp.

Parker, K.F. 1972. *An Illustrated Guide to Arizona Weeds.* The University of Arizona Press, Tucson. 338 pp.

Robbins, W.W., M.K. Bellue, and W.S. Ball. 1970. *Weeds of California.* State of California Documents and Publications, Sacramento. 547 pp.

Weed Science Society of America. 1989. *Composite List of Weeds.* Weed Science Society of America. Weed Science. Vol. 32, Supplement 2. 112 pp.

Whitson, T.D. et al. 1987. *Weeds and Poisonous Plants of Wyoming and Utah.* University of Wyoming Cooperative Extension Service. B-855-UW. Utah State University Cooperative Extension Service and Agricultural Experiment Station. Research Report 116-USU. 282 pp.

Zimdahl, R.L. 1983. *Weeds of Colorado.* Colorado State University Cooperative Extension Service Bulletin No. 521A, Fort Collins. 220 pp.

Index